Crazy Daze

A Bipolar Odyssey

Declan Gould

About the Author

Declan Gould was born in Cork City. Following graduation from UCC as a Civil Engineer, he worked with Cork City Council on the Mahon Design Team.

In 1981 he went to Tennessee, where he lived on "The Farm" International Community, and worked with "Plenty International" development organisation.

After returning to Ireland in 1982, he worked for a time as an officer with "Between" Northern Relief Organisation.

In 1984 he emigrated to Zimbabwe, where he worked as a teacher, and as a rural and urban development worker.

Between 1992 and 1998 he lived in Scotland, where he worked as a surveyor and civil engineer. He returned to Ireland in 1998 to care for his mother. Between 2006 and 2010 he undertook studies in a number of courses in Cork.

In 2010 in Cork, he founded a magazine 'Glenmalure and Friends', later re-branded as "Speak Your Mind", which speaks to people on the margins.

In 2011 he was the inspiration for and founder member of "The Next Step", a voluntary organisation providing creative and engaging activities and workshops for people experiencing emotional difficulties.

Declan continues to live in Cork.

Table of Contents

ISBN:

978-1-716-25579-3
Imprint: Lulu.com

Part 1: Crazy Daze

A Bipolar Odyssey

Foreword

Sanity and insanity are on a continuum and each person occupies a little bit of moving space in that realm. I have been far out towards both extremes and have come to realise that 'normality' and sanity are not always the same thing. For this reason, I have very little to do with a lot of the norms of our society and embrace some, like social justice movements, in particular.

Here is a tale about far-out states of consciousness imbued with a sense of justice and, I hope, humour.

1 - The Farm, Tennessee and Ireland

Stephen

I met Stephen in a Convent in Timoleague, in West Cork, in 1981. He impressed me with his behaviour and his style and, three months later, I decided to move to his Community in Tennessee, where he lived with his wife and fifteen hundred Friends.

The Irish Community in Timoleague had six Americans, their children and a number of Europeans. The Americans were Warren and Barbara; Sam and Ellen; and Francesco and Maria, all of whom I can see clearly in my mind to this day.

Eight years previously, having spent six months working in Belfast Simon Community, I had joined an organisation in London called divine light. I wanted to move forward after my Simon experience and DL held out promise; a promise that was to go disastrously wrong.

I had joined because I had met a young man on the footpath in Huddersfield in England, who told me that he had discovered the meaning of life; that there was a young teenager from India who had "the Knowledge" and he was giving it to true seekers who were in need.

Because I was in that category, I left the City of Huddersfield and headed for London, where I met a 'mahatma', prostrated myself in front of him in tears and asked for 'the Knowledge'.

A few days later, I and a number of other seekers were run through an initiation ceremony, where we were taught four meditation techniques which had extraordinary effects involving the perception of light, nectar and music within; as well as a mantra which had a very soothing effect.

The line being put out by the organisation, was that the guru was 'Lord of the Universe' and that the greatest use to which one could put one's life was in serving him. I went along with it for a while but soon had my doubts.

Even though people gave up drugs and meat when they took up these meditations (we were all vegetarian), there was something about the organisational structure which bothered me. A lot of the practitioners ('premies') lived in ashrams and worked in regular jobs during the day, handing over their pay-checks at the end of the week. Life was simple, but orderly. The guru, on the other hand, lived in a mansion; drove around in a Rolls Royce; and had a Trans Atlantic jet.

Before I got to the point of reservation I was totally head-copped by the organisation and its practices, purely because it had introduced me into levels of consciousness and well-being I had never experienced before. I started writing to my friends about 'lord of the universe'. They were alarmed.

Then reason kicked in. Why should one young teenager and his family be getting all the goodies when the rest of us were doing all the work?

I was in a dilemma; surrounded by premies who were 'blissed out' and talking about the knowledge all the time, and yet knowing that I was propping up an organisation which was a microcosm of the capitalist system.

I didn't have the strength of character to leave because I knew that the knowledge was powerful stuff, but I couldn't square it with my conscience that the guru was the black hole who took all to himself. I started looking for advice from my fellow 'premies' and was advised to ask my questions in meditation.

At this stage the 'knowledge' wasn't working for me so I started meditating harder and longer as well as fasting. I became very unhappy.

One night, I asked a 'mahatma' some question and he said, "Ah, go jump off a bridge". I went to Putney Bridge and was considering my position when a young couple came along. We got talking. When they heard my dilemma they called the local hospital and soon I was in an ambulance, being taken to Banstead, in Sutton, Surrey.

This was a great shock. Sometime earlier I had been searching for God and now I was locked up in the Lunatic Asylum. I was fed with tablets and given electro convulsive therapy and my depression lifted.

Electro-Convulsive Therapy is based on the theory that, because people with epilepsy allegedly don't suffer from depression, if one can give a grand mal seizure to a person suffering from depression, the depression will lift. How crazy that is.

In my case, the ECT wiped out the previous six months of my memory and the doctors told me that was why they had done it. I smell rationalisation here. I lost my memory of most of the preceding six months and when a psychiatrist took me off the tablets, when I got back to Ireland, the blues returned. For a while, in England, I had been in Heaven; but now I had lost it and was in Hell. It's funny how the Universe works.

The psychiatrist then put me on a cocktail of drugs, of his own choosing, which restored me to a level of reasonable functioning. I left St Stephen's Hospital, in a pretty shaky state, trying to put the knowledge, the ashram and the premies behind me.

Dichotomy

While in St Stephen's Hospital I had a seminal experience. I discovered that my mind was whispering two conflicting messages to me: one was to speed up and get on with it and the other was to lay back and to take it easy. It occurred to me that these were messages I had been receiving from my Mother and my Father since I was a kid, because the tenor of these messages corresponded to their respective approaches to reality. To this day I wrestle with these energies.

My Father suggested that, when the new Academic Year would begin, I should return to University to complete my Civil Engineering degree, which I had left two years previously. I acceded to his suggestion and waited for nine months, until the new Academic Year began. In the meantime, my Father placed me in a job, working as a painter in Midleton Hospital in East Cork.

GROW

Another suggestion my Father made was that I should get in touch with an organisation, grandiosely called GROW; the 'Group Rehabilitation Organisation of the World', which recently had opened an office in Cork. My Father had read in the newspaper that this organisation existed for the benefit of people who, like me, had experienced difficult mind trips. It was based in Paul Street and met once per week. I decided to check it out.

There were twenty people at the first meeting and I recognised them as fellow-travellers. Nevertheless it was taking me some time to come around to accepting that I was now part of a social group, which did not enjoy a very high level of acceptance in society. However, as I began to attend meetings and get to know my new friends, I began to realise that they are all real souls and that they, like me, were trying to get straight with each other and God.

I continued to work as a painter; went to the GROW meetings; and, in time, returned to complete my degree. I continued to take tablets and visited St Stephen's monthly, for a ten-minute check-up. However, I eventually felt that I would like to quit the tablets and said this to the psychiatrist on one of my monthly visits.

I had studied for nine hours a few days previously, and the psychiatrist accepted this as evidence of a cure, so I was off the tablets.

Mahon

My first job, having graduated from UCC, was with Waterford Corporation, as an Assistant Resident Engineer on the City Main Drainage Project. The contractor pulled out of the Contract because he had got a better deal elsewhere. I returned to Cork, taking up a job with Cork Corporation, as it was called then, in the Traffic Section. My Section head was weird and gave me a lot of grief so I sought, and was granted, a transfer to the Mahon Design Team.

Mahon Development was to be an Integrated Urban Development and the Mahon Design Team had some very talented architects and engineers on it. I was one of them. I was glad to be a part of the Team because I had a particular interest in Social Development and the Urban Landscape. I worked for four years in Mahon, and then met Stephen.

Haight Street Flashback

In the nineteen sixties, there was a Religious and political foment around the World, particularly in America. The Hippies were on the Spiritual End of this Movement. When I had been in Cape Cod, in

Massachusetts, in 1971, I had hung out with Hippies. They were Spiritual Trippers, investigating the Holy books and discussing them around the table where we worked, in Thompson's Clam Bar in North Truro. I was very impressed by them but returned to pursue my college studies as I was still a square in my Head.

Realisation

A month after meeting Stephen, in Lettercolm House in Timoleague, West Cork, I woke up, one morning and had a flash that I would go to the Farm. I rang Warren, in Timoleague and he told me that he would arrange it.

Timoleague is an Anglicisation of 'Teach Malaga'; the House of Malaga, who was a Celtic Monk who introduced beekeeping into the area.

The folks on The Farm arranged a Visa for me and, in the meantime, I sold my house, left my job, in the process decanting a few other commitments.

The Farm

When I was ready, I took a plane to Nashville via New York and Atlanta and then a bus to Summertown, where The Farm is located. Warren met me off the bus and took me to Thunder Ridge, one of the community houses.

Thunder Ridge was occupied by three Married couples, various Kids and by four Single people. It was one of the biggest Houses on The Farm. At the other end of the scale, there were couples living in some of the school buses which had brought Stephen and 250 of his students onto the 1,700-acre property, years previously.

Poverty was the shared condition of the, by now, 1,500-strong community (if one divided the total income of The Farm businesses by the total population). However, if one added to the equation the on-Farm services, such as the clinic; the Midwifery crew; the soya dairy; the Tempeh (a soya product) Centre; the Store; the Bakery; the Flour Mill; the Bank; the Cropping Area; the Neighbourhood and House Gardens; the Book Publishing Company; the Recording; Television and Radio Stations; the Cable Television Network; the Community horses; the automobiles; the earth-moving equipment; the Farm machinery; the community computers; the wood-shop; and PLENTY (The Farm's Third World Aid project), I found myself in a Rich Environment where money was in the halfpenny place and Love was the currency of the community.

Funds for essentials not produced on The Farm, were earned by the Farm Businesses. These included: Solar Energy Works, the Community Building Company. Right livelihood was the Farm policy and this Company built Solar Houses. There was a Drawing Office adjoining the Wood Shop, where these houses were designed.

Solar Electronics had similar underpinnings. This Company designed user friendly products, which the mainstream electronics companies were overlooking, such as a Doppler foetoscope.

The Food Company developed various flavours of 'ice bean'; a soya-based product and sublet it to national producers

The Book Publishing Company produced books, which were written on The Farm. Topics included: Vegetarian Cooking; the case against the nuclear fuel cycle; CB Radio; Stephen's spiritual teachings; and Midwifery.

Practically every piece of material, from the wood used for the buildings, to the Printing Press and the whole Telephone Exchange were Second-Hand, imported from Off-the-Farm and hauled through the Gate, onto the property.

But, to judge The Farm by the amount of stuff it had, or by the Fact that its Systems worked, would be to miss the point.

When Stephen and his Students set out from San Francisco, in School Buses, in the late Sixties, on a speaking tour of the United States, they did so to make a difference. When, at the end of the tour, he said he was going back to Tennessee to work on the land, they went with him because they believed in his Vision and believed that by working with him and each other, they would make the best possible use of their lives.

So, what was Stephen's vision?

Back in the sixties, through the process of taking hallucinogens, it had become obvious to hundreds of thousands of young Americans that the spiritual;

political; social and dietary underpinnings of their society were built on sand and that a radical rethink was needed.

This was the generation whose parents had lived through the Great Depression and who wanted their children never to experience that hardship. This was the generation, therefore, who made hard work, and security and comfort its main priorities.

Though understandable, it was not enough for their children who gave up College; grew their hair long; left home and went out to see the Country seeking the Truth about what was going on. San Francisco became the beacon for this movement, though it was happening in lots of places.

I met Hippies in Cape Cod, Massachusetts, in the early seventies, and found them to be the sincerest and pleasantest of people. One difference between the Hippy movement and others was that the Hippies' emphasis was on Personal Change, based on Spiritual Values; Non-violence; Vegetarianism and Sharing One's Goods. Non-violence was the force that helped stop the Viet Nam war.

Back in San Francisco, Stephen and some friends started meeting every Monday Night to see if they could come to agreement about the nature of reality. As time went on, more people came, discussing a wide range of topics like Spirituality, Politics and Hallucinogenics. Stephen always had the best handle on things and led the

Meetings, summarising at the conclusion. At the Highest Point, there were over fifteen hundred people in attendance.

A lot of what he spoke about was the unity of consciousness, which arises when a number of people are in agreement or are paying attention to the same information. This experience is ubiquitous: listening to the radio; watching a movie; at plays and concerts. Stephen's gift was one of rare accuracy and honesty added to a very colourful style of communication. He had the ability to raise one's consciousness to an extraordinary level where one felt at one with all one's fellows. I experienced Stephen's ability to change consciousness, in a very agreeable way, in Lettercolm House I experienced it many times, to a greater degree, on The Farm, and have no doubt that that was what was happening in Monday Night Class, in San Francisco, back in the sixties.

The Farm was State of Mind as well as a Social System; what the Tibetans call a Bardo. The elected Elders ran it and Stephen talked it, most Sundays, after Meditation. He called himself 'the coach', and had an uncanny ability of building agreement while thinking and talking on his feet.

He had a saying: "The Farm will get you high, just by paying attention to it."

The Farm had a number of founding principles and staying high was one of them. Another was taking care of each other and the final one was using its surplus to make a contribution to helping the Planet. While I was there I got very high; however, I also had the opposite experience.

Visiting the UN

My highest experience resulted from a letter I received from my Friend, Larry. Larry was editing the magazine, 'Disarmament Today' in Ireland at the time and he wanted an article on why Ireland was voting down anti-nuclear weapons motions which were being sponsored by Third World countries at the United Nations. After talking it over with my Friends in Shangri-La, the house I was living in, I decided to travel to New York and speak to the Irish representative to the UN there. I hitched and, with the assistance of some kind drivers, arrived in New York and went to the United Nations building, where I met a member of the Irish delegation.

On the way, I was standing at the side of a highway when I had a doubt that I was doing the right thing. I asked God for a sign. Immediately, an articulated truck flew passed me, with the name, 'Gould' emblazoned, in bold letters along the side. My doubt passed.

Of course, no-one can prove that events like these are not simply 'coincidences'. But aren't all coincidental events, coincidences. The fact that a force and its opposite occur simultaneously is a coincidence; it's just that it always seems to happen. Other coincidences are one-off and cannot be reproduced under laboratory conditions, so they are relegated to the status of inconsequential.

Back in New York, I headed for the offices of the Irish delegation and went in. I was quite stoned. In the front office I met a quiet spoken man in his forties, who asked me if he could help me and I said that I would like to speak to the Irish delegate. He said that it was he and brought me into his office where we spoke for ten minutes.

I asked him why Ireland was voting down anti-nuclear weapons motions in the General Assembly. He said that they were mischievously inspired to embarrass the nuclear powers. I found this line of argument pretty curious seeing as Ireland had originally sponsored the Nuclear Non-Proliferation Treaty. But I decided not to get into it with him as there was a more pressing issue looming, in the guise of the impending Malvinas crisis. I told him that I thought that Ireland should not support a colonial adventure. He told me that Charlie Haughy had already declared that Ireland would not be supporting Maggie Thatcher's initiative and I said to him that, in that case, he should be speaking out about it in America.

Back to Tennessee
I spent the night in a night shelter for homeless people, which was run by the Office of the Mayor of New York. In the morning, they gave me breakfast and, with the help of money my brother Martin cabled me from St Louis, Missouri, I headed back to Tennessee. On the

way I heard the Irish Delegate on radio, explaining why Ireland would not be supporting Maggie Thatcher.

That evening Mary E, a Friend of mine, asked me to tell her how my trip to New York had gone. We went outside, lit up a joint and I told her my story. When I got to the bit about meeting the Delegate, she said, "You were blessed" and immediately I left my body and all I could see was light.

I felt I was looking at God but I wasn't sure, so I said, "Are You the One?" I had asked Mary E to marry me and she, thinking I was addressing my question to her, said, "I don't know". We started to drift back down to Earth again.

Mary E wanted to talk about what we had just experienced but I, who was very committed to the moment, wanted to let it go and move on.

It can be argued that there was dope, so it didn't count. But I had never had an out-of-body experience and I had never seen light like that, so whether it was Divine or not, it was the most Divine experience of my life.

I paid very close attention to the material plane and the people while I was on The Farm and had many extraordinary psychedelic visions. This wasn't due only to the small quantities of dope I consumed but to the high level of attention I developed. I began to see that the levels of spiritual reality, written of in Holy Books, could be experienced in my own lifetime. This frightened me, because I realised also that these levels of reality called for a degree of heroism, which I had never aspired to, or rather manifested, in my life.

At the same time, a lot of negative feelings about my Family started to come into my awareness and prevented me from speaking honestly about what I was seeing in front of myself, or about my Family. I felt that if I spoke about my Family I would cry, and so I stayed silent a lot of the time; an Irish trait, which we are getting out of fast.

One of the consequences of being stoned is that one realises there are energy 'conversations' going on constantly, between different parts of the body. In normal consciousness this stuff is subconscious, but in a stoned condition this fact is quite apparent. Talking about it is one effective way of dealing with it.

I stayed on The Farm for a year. I knew that my Father had gone into hospital for a cataract operation and, within days of hearing the news, I had an auditory Vision that my Father was going to die and that if I didn't get back to Ireland, I would never see him alive.

I rang David, the Banker, and he picked me up, drove me to the Airport, gave me a ticket and saw me off. I knew that I had been living with Saints and had a job to do in spreading the word. What I wasn't allowing for was my own condition.

2 – Back in Ireland
Ireland

While I had been on The Farm I had been quiet – in the fastest-talking community I had ever experienced. I had also had many high and low experiences. Now I was high, determined to stay so, and also to do some fast-talking. What I didn't realise was that my energy was out of kilter and that I looked very weird to my friends. They kept away. My Family also tore me apart.

My Father was in the Eye, Ear and Throat Hospital, on the Western Road and I visited him with my Family. When I saw him, I had a very high thought – long since forgotten – but was afraid to voice it, lest I disturb the ambience. Instead, I opted for a lower-level truth and immediately my Father threw up which I took to be a sign of his disgust at my chicken-heartedness.

I went outside the hospital and decided there was nothing I could do for my Father and that the best thing I could do would be to return to The Farm. Having four pounds in my pocket I would work my passage, on a ship, so I went home to pack my bags.

As I was ready to go, my Family arrived and prevented me from leaving. My brother rang Stephen and asked him was I welcome on the Farm. Stephen said that I was, but that I should make better plans and not to leave without my Family's agreement. He was covering his bases well.

Ellen's Cottage

My Father was dead and buried and I discovered that I had to attend to some unfinished business, involving Ellen Daly's cottage.

Back in the nineteen seventies, Ellen had lived in a two-roomed cottage on the Boreenmanna Road, next to Flower Lodge Stadium, before it became Páirc Uí Rinn. She was disabled and spent most of her time in bed. Her cottage had a galvanised iron roof, no sanitation and an earthen floor.

Before going to The Farm, I had met 'Nellie', on a Meals-on Wheels round with my Mother. Nellie had told me that her dream was to have a new house. I said I would build her one.

I drew up plans with the help of a good friend on the Mahon Design Team; negotiated a disability Grant from Cork Corporation; found some volunteer workers in the community and work began. Donal Counihan, who later would become Lord Mayor of Cork; Jack Healy; Dermot Kelly; the MacNamara kids; were the most active in our group. My Father and his Brother, Jack, joined us later with a retired fitter, who had returned from the United States.

To get started, we had to find £400, because the Corporation wouldn't pay the first instalment of the Grant until one quarter of the work had been done, so Nellie put up the money. A Quaker friend, who owned a Builders' Suppliers depot, also supplied some building materials on credit. Nellie's £400 injection was to lead to some tussling with Ballinlough Community Association.

When the work was done and Nellie had moved back into the cottage (we had done a renovation), she decided that she would like to leave it to some organisation, which would maintain it for the benefit of old people in Ballinlough. She engaged a solicitor to advise her.

The solicitor advised her to give it to the parish priest, so that he could manage it. I was against this, as the parish priest had no connection with the project and as I also had some latent anti-Catholic feelings, arising out of aspects of my education.

I had an argument with the solicitor about this and she retired her brief.

The Community Association – some of whose members had been involved in the renovation – expressed an interest in taking over the property and I told Nellie that I thought that this was appropriate. Ellen agreed and laid three conditions: the Association would reimburse her for her £400 outlay; she would be guaranteed life tenancy and the Association would hold the property in perpetuity, in Trust for old people in the Parish. The Association agreed. At that point I left for The Farm.

When I got back from The Farm a year later, I visited Nellie and she told me that the money hadn't been passed over. I approached the chairman of the Association and he denied that any deal had been made about the money. Next I went to the community council

and the secretary blew smoke in my face. Clearly, I was
being stonewalled so I decided to fast, in order to draw
them out.

I called into 'Cork Local Radio' and spoke to a reporter.
At lunchtime, we were on radio with a Councillor,
representing the Association. I was pretty feeble because
I didn't want to get into public disagreement with an
organisation with which I was trying to get accord. The
reporter told me afterwards that it hadn't been good
radio. However, the Association went back to their
records. They found that the agreement to pay Nellie
the money had, in fact, been made so the money was
passed over. Then Nellie decided that she wanted the
garden done as well, so I did the garden.

The Association took over the cottage and Nellie lived
in it until she died.

Then a new tenant came in and the Association out of
generosity, but unwisely, charged him a very low rent.
The tenant would not let them onto the property for
maintenance purposes and the property ran down.
Eventually the tenant died and the Association did not
have enough money to repair it. I asked for a meeting,
with the Association to discuss the matter and my
request was ignored. The property then lay idle and in
disrepair. The promise that the Association, at their
request, made to Nellie Daly, to hold her cottage in
Trust for the benefit of old people in Ballinlough was
conveniently forgotten. Perhaps it would have been

better to give the cottage to the parish priest; he might
have been more likely to keep his word.

A couple of years ago, Nellie's house was taken over by
Cork Mental Health Housing Association. They razed it
to the ground and built a replacement. The house is now
part of their housing stock which is for the benefit of
people in need who are experiencing mental health
difficulties. A good solution finally.

Nellie Daly and the Sun
In order to promulgate Nellie's case at the time that the
Association owed her £400, I went to the Catholic
church, on a Sunday morning. My plan was to tell
people coming out of Mass, about her situation. I was
hallucinating heavily and, in my open-minded state,
was able to look at the sun, without blinking.

As I was talking to this lady, I kept my eyes on the sun
and it seemed like the sun was telepathically telling me
what to say. These messages kept coming and then I got:
"I am the Son of God". At that point, I stopped
speaking. "I am _a_ son of God" would have presented
me with no problem but not wanting to be incarcerated
for violating the spiritual and social orthodoxies, I
walked away. I was very high in those days, but the
internal tracking system was also functioning.

Paint
My Father had been buried in St Joseph's Cemetery,
near Ballyphehane and Friar's Walk , and I started

taking an interest in the community again, having been in the States for a year.

The story was going around Cork that a man in the City had been falsely claiming social welfare payments and that someone had reported him. The story was that the false claimant, believing he knew who had denounced him, went around Cork City painting his denouncer's name and address, with details of the perceived treachery, on walls in various parts of the City. I felt that he was acting as judge and jury and decided to do something about it.

My first move was to contact the assistant City manager. I had known him from my time in the scouts. He wasn't interested. So I bought a can of paint, a brush and got to work.

One of the messages was on the outside wall of the men's toilet, on the South Mall – now gone. In my engineering days, with the traffic section of the Cork Corporation, I had spray painted the footpath outside the toilet, to indicate the positions of cables. Now I was painting the toilet - not the normal career path.

Next I went to a lane off The Grand Parade, and got creative by turning each letter of the counter-denunciation into a flower. As I was working, a squad car pulled up and the Gardaí asked me what I was doing. I told them the story, including my telephone call with the assistant city manager, and that did it; they drove away. Being men of justice, they realised that an act of injustice had been committed and could see that it was being attended to.

Auditory Hallucination

Anyone who has seen the film 'Monty Python and the Holy Grail' will probably remember the scene where Arthur is riding along on his steed, when the skies open. God appears and speaks to him.

I had one of those experiences when riding my bike to Carrigaline, to see my Aunt and her Husband. As I was cycling down Carr's Hill approaching Carrigaline, I said to myself that I would do anything for World Peace. Immediately I heard the loud voice of God, which said, "If you want to do something for World Peace, cycle naked to Cork". I was horrified, thinking of the humiliation of it and I questioned God's order. He reminded me of what I had just said to myself and, with resignation I cycled to my Aunt's house to leave my clothes.

Mounting my bike, I headed for Cork and tried to keep my mind off of my surroundings and the possibility that people might be watching. I knew that I was in Catholic territory and that the agents of the State might be in the vicinity. For some reason I stopped at a petrol station to make a phone call and then carried on with my journey. Minutes later, a squad car pulled up.

The two occupants got out and one threw my bike over the ditch while the other threw me into the car. We drove to Cork.

On the way I said that I would like to be dropped off at the Franciscans, in Liberty Street and the Guards headed in that direction. For some reason, as we approached the Franciscans, I let out an oath and, immediately, the Guards changed direction and headed for the Bridewell Garda Station, on Cornmarket Street. I felt that my halo had slipped and, as a consequence, my captors decided that it was not a matter for the Church; it was a matter for the State. We arrived at the station.

When we got to the station, I was given a blanket and the Bean Garda behind the counter started laughing. I was shown to a cell.

I decided that I would generate some good vibrations and chose Jack Marinan as my topic. He was the President of the Garda Representative Association at the time, and I had a lot of time for him. Being gifted musically and with a fair talent for doggerel rhythm I launched into a series of songs in praise of Jack and things seemed to be going well because, every so often, one of the Guards would pass by and say, "Great voice. Great voice".

This was the effect I wanted until, suddenly, it seemed like I was becoming an exhibit in some sort of show. I could hear this lady, who had been in one of the adjacent cells, asking a Guard if she could see me. He obliged and opened the hatch on my cell door. She looked and I could immediately see that her focal point was my crotch. It was an education in female sexuality.

Auditory hallucinations, as they have come to be known, are well documented in the Texts, going back thousands of years. In our own times we have Lourdes, Fatima, Garabandal, Knock; and we have our sceptics and our adherents. I'm not suggesting that we set up an Annual Pilgrimage to Carrigaline but I am saying that when one has the experience I had there, it is terrifying and disobedience is not an option. There has to be order in the Universe.

As for the purpose or meaning of this, I have no idea. I do believe in a Transcendent Being, relative to which I am but an atom. The only conclusion I can draw is that, if I am an atom, I'll be spinning forever, without really knowing why. The main thing, I guess, is not to bump into other atoms.

Concilio

I was still living with my Mother and Brothers in Ballinlough. One afternoon on the landing I could see a light in front of me, calling me to go to Sr. Concilio's community in Athy, Co Kildare. Within twenty four hours, I was on the road.

An actor with the Everyman Theatre picked me up near St Patrick's church, on the Lower Glanmire Road, and drove me as far as the Tivoli Roundabout. Because I was celibate, I told him that I was a monk; but I subsequently felt quite embarrassed about that statement because I realised that being a monk is a heavy calling and I had simply been talking off the top of my head.

I reached this village at dusk, and there were two butchers standing outside the door of their shop. I asked them the way to Cuan Mhuire and they told me how to get there. As I left them, I could see droplets of blood on their skin and thought it was coming from within them. I knew I was on a bad trip.

It was getting late and dark and this guy stopped and picked me up. I must have been in a pretty vulnerable state because I could feel him getting inside my head and there was nothing I could do about it. I was colonised, in spite of my greatest efforts to evacuate him. Then he started talking about disease and his theories on how to get rid of it. "You can pass it on", he said, and, as he did so, he slapped my thigh and a bolt of electricity shot up through it. I asked him to stop the car and staggered out of it, trying to get myself together. I knew that I was in poor shape psychically, but saw Cuan Mhuire as a refuge and I was determined to get there.

An English guy stopped to pick me up and we got into conversation. I decided to introduce him to a few Irish songs, in a kind of hospitable gesture and told him that I was glad that things were getting better between the two islands. He told me that he didn't like the Irish, which kind of took the wind out of my sails. I realised that my evening trip to Concilio's wasn't going well.

This couple picked me up as they were travelling home from a function. He was a very quiet guy and, consequently, the lady and I did all the talking. Then she said to me, "I should have taken you instead of him", which I thought was a pretty lousy thing to say and I felt for her companion's feelings. They left me off.

The moon was up and I was getting close, out on a country road. I looked at the moon and felt like my brain was being sand-blasted by it; a hot, searing sensation streaming through the top of my head; a very unpleasant feeling. I tried a few experiments with it and tried to control it but there was nothing I could do about it. I had looked at the moon hundreds of times throughout my life, but had never experienced anything like this. I decided that I must have changed – the moon looked the same – and decided that it must be some form of lunacy; whatever that is.

It is well-known that the moon affects the tides and menstrual cycles but whatever happened to me that night was awful and so, keeping my eyes firmly on the Planet I walked on until I tried to go to sleep on the verge at the side of the road.

Not succeeding I resumed hitching and was picked up by a group of young adults, including this lady who told me that she worked in the bank near Cuan Mhuire. I told her that I was going there. As I was alighting from the car near my destination she told me that, if I was in the bank, I should not mention that I had met her. Reeling from this nugget of social orthodoxy, I walked on.

I reached my destination: Cuan Mhuire - the harbour of Mary – and knocked on the door. One of the residents listened to my story and, when I had finished, took me to a bunk bed in one of the dormitories.

Then I realised that if I stayed, I would be hassling Concilio to change the community diet to vegetarianism and to adopt solar energy, which, I decided would not be a good idea seeing as it was her community and it had to be run her way. I headed back for Cork by train.

Some weeks later I was back, in a new frame of mind. I spent the next few weeks walking rapidly around the community, talking to all and sundry about solar and vegetarianism; until, one day I saw this guy walking purposefully across an open space at the back of the main building. He had his eyes fixed straight ahead, hands down by his side; straight back. He was me; that was how I was moving around the place. Seeing him took a bit of wind out of my sails; I changed my tack.

One day, this guy, who had come from a primal screaming community in the northwest, attacked me, grabbing me by the throat and throwing me back onto my back. I wrapped my legs around his torso, tickled him with my feet and he let me go. I left the scene, fast, with as much composure as I could muster.

Life in Concilio's community was punctuated by work, meals, prayers and meetings, at which practical matters were discussed. She had a right-hand man and I thought that he wasn't doing his job well. Indiscreetly, I told him this, as we were waiting for the beginning of a meeting. We started to argue. Concilio came in; saw what was going on and said, "We'll say a 'Hail Mary'. End of argument. Neither of us was prepared to oppose the power of prayer.

Synchronicity

I was having intimations that I should leave Cuan Mhuire. One day I was in the oratory, maybe meditating, maybe saying a prayer. In came this sister and, in a very agitated state, started praying for forgiveness. In a rather unfeeling way, I laughed and told her that her prayers were unnecessary because she was forgiven already.

Each night, the community said the Rosary. Most of the people there were men. It was customary for the men to crouch on one knee. I used to keep my back straight during the prayers and experienced very intense energy in my spine during these sessions. I said it to the men one night, but they weren't interested; it was hard enough for them to keep it together as it was, without me laying my kundalini trip on them.

Within days, I was gone, travelling northward. I reached this town and walking through it, I saw a nun, with her back to me. I walked up to her, to tell her that I had been in Cuan Mhuire. As I reached her, she turned around and who was it? The penitent sister from the oratory. I'm sure she has long since gotten over it.

Special Powers

Symbols are endemic on our Planet and, often, the slightest misinterpretation can make all the difference in the world.

Being in an elevated state of mind, my internal GPS system could ascertain only that I was in Connaught. It was a bright sunny morning. I had my rucksack on my back, walking along a country road and I was in love with the world.

I saw a Garda squad car up ahead, with a Garda next to it. As an act of peace I raised my right palm; facing in his direction and arranged my index and second fingers in a 'V'-configuration. This is the international Peace sign but he appeared to misinterpret it because he grabbed me and threw me into the back of his car and drove me to the Garda Station.

I asked what the charge was and he said that he was arresting me under the Offences Against the State Act, but refused to specify what section. I think it was the section covering his ego.

We arrived at the Station and my captor indicated a seat and started questioning me with less than a friendly demeanour. The Sergeant came in; a tall, grey-haired, genial-looking man and asked what was going on. I explained and the sergeant left. Minutes later he returned, carrying a tray of tea and scones – from his wife; they lived next-door. He told me to tuck in.

While I was eating this unexpected breakfast, I talked
with the Sergeant and my captor looked on in silence.
When I had consumed the meal, the Sergeant and I
talked a little more and then, it seemed to me that it
would be OK for me to go.

I got up from my seat and headed for the door and my
captor grabbed me and threw me back into my
seat…further conversation with the Sergeant.

Eventually, my captor stormed out in bad grace and,
this time, I knew I could go. I headed for the door and
the Sergeant went with me and gave me directions to
my next destination.

Heavy Karma

One sunny evening, on the outskirts of Castlebar in
County Mayo, I was walking along this country road,
with no goal in mind, when I came upon this lone
trailer, parked on the side of the road. I formed the
opinion that, maybe, the occupant was lonely and could
need cheering up. I crossed the road to the trailer;
knocked on the door, but there was no reply. I walked
on.

Some minutes later, a Garda patrol car pulled by and I
was taken in for questioning. So used was I to this
pattern in my life, that I didn't ask why and we got to
the Garda Station.

My interrogator came in and proved to be a pleasant
man; a plain clothes officer. He started asking me
detailed questions about myself, which I didn't enjoy. I

decided to change the centre-of-gravity of the conversation and started asking him questions about himself and his family. He was generous enough to share that information and pretty soon, I was released back onto the roads of County Mayo.

A year later, I was talking to this lady, from Castlebar and told her my story. She said there had been a murder there when I had been there, and it was obvious that the Gardaí had been looking for the murderer. I'm glad that my encounter with them had ended on a friendly note.

Religious Zeal

During my travels in Rural Ireland, I often had the feeling (especially at night), that I was travelling through the past, as often there was a lack of twentieth century icons in the environment.

One day, as I was walking, I came upon a Catholic church and decided to go in and seek Holy Orders from the Creator. I prostrated myself in the aisle; made my request and left.

Later that night, as I happened upon a small, one storey farm house, it seemed as if I was back in Famine times. I crept into the shed at the back of the farm house and settled in. Soon, I realised I was hungry. I knocked at the farmer's back door and whispered in that I was a priest and that I needed some bread, to say Mass. There was a slight delay and then, the door opened slightly and a hand appeared, holding two slices of white bread, which I took with thanks, before leaving for the shed.

Back in the shed, I realised that I hadn't a clue how to say Mass, as the transmission hadn't contained that information. In any case, I was very hungry, so I ate my two slices of white bread and went to sleep; getting up and leaving, the following day.

Smile

It's a funny thing that the body, sometimes, doesn't want to do what the Mind wants it to do. It's as if our internal wiring isn't complete and that we are still trying to get full control of the organism. I had an experience, like that in County Mayo.

Having travelled on foot all day, I came to a farmhouse in the evening and quietly went around to the shed and lay down on the straw, for a night's rest.

In the morning I awoke, but was too lazy to get up and carry on with my journey. I had a premonition that, if I didn't leave, the farmer would come out and challenge me, but still, I couldn't get it together to collect myself and disappear from the scene.

Sure enough, the farmer appeared, carrying a pitchfork and let me know that if I didn't vacate his property, forthwith, some of the pitchfork would be embedded in my flesh. I rose, immediately and headed for the nearby road, followed closely by the farmer, holding the business end of his implement a centimetre from my back.

I could have just walked on, along the road outside his farm, but, for some reason, turned and started talking to him. I think that I was trying to show him that I wasn't afraid of him and kept smiling all the time I was talking to him. I deduced that, if I kept smiling at him, he wouldn't jab me, because a smile is a very powerful form of defence (witness the actors who waltz in and out of these periodic Tribunals of Enquiry).

However, I decided that the smile was getting a bit unreal and dropped it, at which point the pitchfork penetrated my chest with my farmer friend's assistance. I did leave at that point, because unnecessary suffering has no justification, and walked into the day.

As for sleeping on farmer's property, I wouldn't do it now; unless he said it was OK, of course.

Fatherhood

The bond between a father and son is not measured by the physical conditions in which they live, but in the feelings that keep them together.

At this stage on my journey, I was feeling hungry a lot of the time and was grateful, one evening in County Mayo, to meet a man who lived in a cottage, with his son, on the side of the road I was travelling on. He invited me in for a cup of tea and some bread. As I ate and drank, he gave instructions to his son, concerning his chores and soon it was time for me to leave. I thanked him and left.

Walking away from the house, I realised I had a packet of biscuits in my bag. I headed back to give them biscuits as an expression of my gratitude to them, for the generosity they had shown me. On my way back, I met the son and offered him the biscuits. The father came along and shouted at me to clear off. Whether he was being protective towards his son or I had now reached Tramp status, I know not.

Righteous Indignation

Righteous Indignation is a dicey business; it can get out of control. Here's a story, where it happened to me, in County Mayo.

Being in the vicinity of a Convent, I decided to call and commune with some kindred spirits. I was greeted at the door, invited into the parlour and offered tea and scones. Some time later I left and resumed my journey.

Some minutes later, a car pulled up and the driver offered me a lift. I saw that there was a sister in the back seat and got into conversation with her, about renewable energy.

I had been in the Irish Anti-Nuclear Movement when the Government had proposed to build a nuclear power station, at Carnsore Point, in County Wexford. The Movement had become so widespread that the Government changed its mind and decided not to build. An accident at Three Mile Island power station, and recognition that the costs would be huge, had also influenced this decision. But, in the process of my involvement with the Movement, I had come to realise that renewable energy was the way forward, for a clean energy future.

As the sister and I were talking, to my amazement I saw
that there was a large wind turbine alongside us, in a
field. I asked the driver to stop the car and got out,
intent on finding out more about this wind turbine.

I estimated, from the diameter of the blades, that it had
a generation capacity of about 0.5 Megawatts but saw
that, though the wind was blowing, the blades were
static.

I wanted to know why because this was obviously a test
model for an electricity production system, which could
have radical implications for Irish society. As luck
would have it, there was an electricity generating station
about 100 metres away and, clearly they would be
responsible for monitoring and maintaining the turbine.

I called in and spoke to one of the engineers and he told
me that maintenance was handled by the Dublin office
and he gave me the number, which I rang, speaking to
the engineer-responsible.

I was very angry, because I thought he wasn't getting
out the finger, when national energy security was at
stake. I told him that the Anti Nuke Movement hadn't
been for nothing and that he should fix the machine,
immediately.

Whether he did, or not, I do not know, but, some thirty
five years later, this country is still hugely dependent on
imported oil and gas for its electricity generation; prices
are rising all the time and security of supply is
becoming shakier. Meanwhile, our wind-generated

electricity sector now makes up about 40% of capacity, but with no opportunity to store the electricity generated, when supply outstrips demand. We need hydrogen storage because with hydrogen storage, this country could be totally self-sufficient in electricity production.

My Rucksack

As I was walking along, with my rucksack on my back, I came upon a rural bungalow. There was an old man in the garden, tending to the flowers. A young man, who I decided was his son-in-law, came out of the house and spoke unkindly to him. In my strange state of mind, I concluded that the old man was unhappy (probably true, at that moment), and that he wanted to leave home. (Maybe I thought he wanted to do what I was doing).

I decided to help him and left my rucksack, at the gate to his bungalow, to help him on his way. I walked on, with nothing but my cloths, committing myself to Jesus as I went. Little did I know that some time later I would be committed, in another setting.

Fr. McDyer

I was in the Glencolmcille area, in County Donegal. I knew that Fr McDyer and his people had been planning on pooling all the land in their area, and running it as one thing. I wanted to know how the project was going so I headed for Glencolmcille on a Sunday afternoon. I arrived at the dressing rooms of the local GAA Club, as the players were dressing after a game.

I asked them how the project was progressing and, laughing, they said it had been called off. Feeling disappointed, I left, to the sound of their laughter.

A Borderline Case

Planet Earth, seen from outer space, displays no political borders.

At one point on my journey I was heading north, in the Republic, on a minor country road. I knew that I was approaching the 'border' but could see no evidence of it; the fields and ditches were continuous; there was no change in the colour scheme of nature.

Then I came on the evidence; a lone British soldier, standing on the road at an intersection, supported by another gun-wielding soldier, in a pill-box. I approached them.

The standing soldier asked me to raise my arms, so that he could frisk me. In order to equalise the relationship, I started to frisk him, all the time talking to him, in a friendly way, so as not to alarm him. I told him that he wouldn't be in Ireland, frisking me, if he could have got a job in his own country. Luckily for me, he found this highly amusing and there we were, in the middle of the road, 'doing the frisk', together, while his gun-toting colleague looked on, in silence, from his box.

A car approached and parked in front of us. The occupants were watching the whole thing. Lest the soldier feel embarrassed to be seen fraternising with a civilian, I gently manoeuvred him out of sight of the car and we finished the ritual in private. Then I left and walked into Northern Ireland.

I didn't go very far before deciding that this wasn't for me. I decided to turn back. Of course this brought me, again, to the check point and, this time the pill-box man's gun was pointing directly at me. Then I did something dumb and dangerous.

I had been eating an apple and, in an act of Peace, I silently offered it to the pill-box man, his gun pointing directly at my head. Luckily I got away with it and headed back into the Republic.

Nabbed

When high, it can seem that one is outside the Law; one is not. Having walked for a few days, I reached Donegal Town and looked around.

First, I met a bunch of teenagers and told them of the coming IT revolution. After this, I called to a local restaurant and asked for a complimentary meal, which the proprietor provided. I was grateful and thanked him a number of times. He said, "Don't be over-weaning, in your gratitude, lest you embarrass the giver."

I knew I shouldn't hang around Donegal Town. I got talking to this guy in the Square and he told me that he was about to drive a few miles out of town, in my direction, and that he would give me a lift. We headed for his car. On our way, he decided that a pint would be a good start to the journey, so I left him and walked out of town by myself.

The Youth Hostel came into view and I approached it. I went in and sat down with these people, in the Common Room. This American guy was describing to the others, a meal he had had on a previous occasion. He had a very lecherous expression in his voice as if he was reliving every bite in front of all the others, who were listening quietly and hanging on every word.

I asked if anyone could make a donation to the price of a bed for the night. No one was giving. A little disappointed at the absence of traveller solidarity, I went upstairs to the dormitory. My logic was that I was God's creature, there were plenty spare beds and it could rain for the night. Therefore, I concluded, there was no Law in the Universe that said I couldn't occupy a bed. However, the warden obviously disagreed; came in; gave me a roasting and left. This may have contributed to the karma I was to face the following day.

The following day I was back in the town. Without paying, I picked up a couple of bags of trail mix outside a Health Food Shop. My standards were sliding and the payload was imminent.

Later, I went into a supermarket and helped myself to an orange. The proprietor was onto me in a flash. He grabbed me and called the Gardaí, who, as luck would have it, were parked just down from the shop. I was bundled into the squad car and, within minutes, we were in the Station.

The previous day, as I had passed the Station, I had come across a garden gnome on the ground. Because the Station was closed, I had left the gnome on one of its windowsills, lest the owner return looking for it.

Now that I was back in the Station, as a captive, I saw that the Gardaí had given the gnome pride-of-place in the room and had installed it on the mantelpiece.

I was given a chair, but didn't talk; instead I meditated on the gnome (bad move).

Some time later, one of the Gardaí told me that there was a doctor waiting to see me in the interview room. I went in and the doctor was sitting, smoking a cigarette. I made my second bad call and decided to keep the conversation off me and on his smoking instead.

As he questioned me, I kept alluding to his habit and this irritated him. He told me that he was sending me to a psychiatric hospital. I was put in a squad car and driven to Letterkenny Hospital.

A few days before, I had gone to Mass and had found the sermon to be boring so I had left. Now that my accompanying Gardaí and I were in Letterkenny Hospital, a male nurse met us in the foyer. He took one look at me and said, "Oh, you're the guy who walked out of Mass last Sunday!" It may have been an innocent remark, but at the time I took it as an accusation that I had been stepping out of line and that, therefore, I was probably in the right place.

I was shown to a bed in a closed ward; my home for the next two weeks, housing about twenty men. Across the ward from me was a guy, who was so into the moment that he couldn't decide what to do next. He was lying still, on his bed. He called across to me, asking if he should move his leg and I said yes. He moved his leg and lay still, again.

I was a vegan at the time and asked for vegan food. The kitchen wasn't geared up for vegan dishes so they gave me the usual potato and veg and the protein component was supplied in the form of sponge cake. It was primitive in those days; maybe it still is.

I spent the following two weeks, locked in the ward, performing hundreds of press-ups and circumnavigating the premises, many times, at speed; all to keep me active, both physically and mentally. Eventually the taxi arrived.

I had mixed feelings about the taxi. Letterkenny had got in touch with Cork and, as I was on the books in Cork, two male nurses were dispatched by taxi, to pick me up in Letterkenny and bring me back to Cork.

My mixed feelings arose from my perception that the taxi was a bit extravagant and that a bus would have done the job. However I was glad to be leaving Letterkenny Hospital. We travelled to Cork where I spent some time in St Stephen's Hospital, until it was deemed that I was ready for freedom, again.

No Go NATO

George Bush Senior, the US Vice-President, was in Ireland, trying, among other things, to persuade the Irish Government to join NATO. A number of my CND Friends and I, not seeing eye-to-eye with George, decided that we would express our displeasure at his presence in our country, by holding an all-night Vigil on the steps of the US embassy.

The day after the Vigil, George was due to lay a wreath at the Garden of Remembrance, where people who died for the Independence of Ireland are laid. I thought that this was a bit ironic. The Vigil people decided to engage in some protest action and got into discussion, as to what format it might take. They decided to mount a silent protest at the Garden of Remembrance.

It is a cardinal principle of non-violent protest that decisions are made by consensus. I was looking for something a bit more action-orientated and I left the group, moving to Upper O'Connell Street where George was due to pass in cavalcade, planning to sit in front of his car.

A second principle of non-violent, direct action, is that one always announces one's intentions in advance and, being more principled then than I am now, that's what I did. I approached a superintendent and told him that I intended to sit in front of George Bush's car and, for the first time in my life, I saw the face of fascism.

Glowering down at me, he dug his heel into my toe, and held it there for a few moments, while uttering an oath through his teeth. He then raised his foot. End of communion.

I realised that, in order to augment my effort, I should have the media present to capture the moment where the Irish people said 'No to NATO', and headed for the, nearby offices of the Dublin County Council. This was before Dublin County Council was divided into three entities. My idea was to ask the secretary there to call the 'Irish Times' and ask them to send a photographer along for the sit-in.

Unknown to me, the secretary called the Gardaí, instead, because, when I got to the bottom of the stairs of the Council Offices, there was a Garda, waiting to arrest me.

I guess the technical term for it would have been, 'intent to commit a breach of the peace', but, in any case, the Garda couldn't find his pencil and had to borrow one from a nearby colleague.

He and two colleagues drove me to the Bridewell On the way, we laughed at the lost pencil incident; a mutual recognition of human fallibility.

When we got to the Station, I was shown to a large cell, in which there were about ten others. I started talking extemporaneously, and one wasted-looking guy, seeing my long hair and beard, sat in front of me and moaned, "You talk like Jesus". Another guy standing behind him, put his hands to his ears and moaned, "I can't stand this!" (referring to me). I shut up.

The Gardaí kept moving me from cell-to-cell and I got the impression that they were moving all of us around, all of the time to prevent tension-build-up; but, maybe, it was just me. There is an underground tunnel connecting the Bridewell to an adjacent building where the District Court is located. I was in another cell when the door opened yet again, and I was led along a corridor, through this tunnel and up a narrow stairs, not into another cell, but into the courtroom. My case was already half over and I had not been present. The judge had already heard the arresting Garda's evidence and, when I appeared, asked me if I wanted to cross-examine the Garda. I was beginning to ask myself who was writing the script for my life.

If I had my wits about me, I would have asked to hear the evidence but, being knocked off balance by the intimidating design of the setting and the circumstances in which I found myself, I let it suffice to ask the arresting Garda if I had been honest and if I had been co-operative with him. He answered, in the affirmative, to both these questions, at which point the judge said, "I am willing to accept that you are of good character; thirty pounds or thirty days". I remained silent, knowing that I wasn't going to pay the thirty pounds and believing that I wasn't going to do the thirty days.

I was released from custody and met my arresting officer in the yard outside the Court. I shook hands with him and thanked him for his honourable conduct. A colleague standing behind him, said, "Well done". I think he was talking to the Garda. The colleague had permanent tears streaming down his face and I deduced that it was from a life observing constant injustice. Of course, it may have been a medical condition. I'm just saying what I thought, at the time.

Also I have thought many times since, of the poor, inarticulate men and women who face the unsympathetic system of reproach daily, while articulate merchants get away with bribing politicians for rezoning 'favours' and smile all the way into and out of the Tribunals, knowing that they have the system sown up; and the politicians who cash in their votes for hard currency; they and those who gain the World and lose their Souls, as George Harrison said.

Footnote: Whether the Garda system fouled up or my arresting officer pulled the documentation, I have no idea, but I didn't hear from the Gardaí in Dublin again and I neither paid the thirty pounds nor spent thirty days in prison. However, Ireland continues to be courted by NATO. It's a case of 'Beauty and the Beast', and the Beast is making inroads. "We're Neutral, but we will allow American soldiers on their way to war, to land in Shannon. We are Neutral, but we will join NATO's Partnership for Peace". It's really Neutrality for the non-Neutral because we don't want to be isolated; which is a new word for 'Independent'.

Spirits

Another manifestation of the friendship that exists between the Irish and the American people (I've been to America, I know what it's like), was when Ronald Reagan came to Ballyporeen, Co Tipperary, to commune with his ancestral spirits, who, he said, resided there.

Ronnie's government had got its hands dirty in Central America, supporting right wing death squads, and a number of Church and Secular Peace Groups felt he should not be let get away with a media coup, using Irish television and deceased Irish people as his allies. We planned a march. It was advertised nationally, though the organising group came from Cork.

Such is the friendship between the Irish and the American people that it had been deemed by the Irish government, in advance of the visit, that any protest to it would not be broadcast until the visit was over. The government apparently felt that the American people, all of whom supported their President, would have been offended to see their Irish friends objecting to some of their country's foreign policy. And, of course, the Americans didn't have The First Amendment, guaranteeing the right to freedom of speech?

Some of the organisers (including me), who had been part of the Irish Anti-Nuclear Movement, were concerned that the march be non-violent. We had seen the loony left hijack a march in Dublin and it hadn't been a pretty sight.

To ensure order and peaceful protest we imported a method, developed in Mr Reagan's own country, by his more enlightened compatriots. This was the method of affinity groups.

As each busload of protestors arrived, it was taken aside and introduced to its leader. People introduced themselves; tactics were discussed and the group joined the march with a loose idea of what to expect and how to behave.

The march on Ballyporeen started and eventually we came to a cordon. We felt very weird to see that a US secret service guy, through a Garda interpreter, was running it.

This other guy and I had a banner commemorating the people who had died in Central America, which we proposed to unfurl in front of the television cameras, while Ronald spoke. It was hidden at the bottom of a shopping basket, which we presented to the Garda for him to search. He searched it, didn't find the banner and we were past the checkpoint and a few hundred metres from the square in the village.

When we got to the square where Ronald was to speak, there was a crowd, about three-deep, arrayed behind the barriers. Foolishly, my friend and I tried to get through to the front, to unfurl our barrier. Sensing our intent, in a loud voice, a woman said, "Here come the troublemakers". We retreated.

There was a platform near us, with a television camera and a commentator in it; the RTE commentary box. I caught the commentator's attention and told him of the banner, hoping he would get the cameraman to cover it. Rather apologetically, he explained that the government ran RTE and that the government had said, "No protest". With this piece of democratic orthodoxy ringing in our ears, we unfurled the banner anyway and were immediately jumped on by four of our men in blue, who took the banner, bundled it up and moved away again. We returned to the march.

Ronald finished his address and left. The march moved towards the village square and, while it was a bit like 'after the horse has bolted', we put on a good show; chanted our chants and remembered the dead in Central America, before turning back, leaving a few onlookers to register the fact that we had exorcised Ronald's demons.

Adi Roche was the March negotiator for that march and she was so good at it that the guy in charge of the Guards offered her a job. She turned it down and went working for the kids of Chernobyl instead.

Fast
It was a few days before Hiroshima Day and the Lord Mayor had come to open an Anti-Nuclear exhibition, sponsored by CND, at the Cork City Library. He began his speech. I agreed with some of it and didn't agree with some of it.

In order to let him know where I was at, I would either nod or shake my head, every time he looked in my direction. He soon got wind of what was going on and started to lose his composure, becoming ragged in his delivery.

In retrospect, I don't know why I did that but my consciousness was at ceiling level and, in the middle of his speech, had the notion that I should fast for forty days for Peace. The reference is obvious and I wasn't sure I could do it but I was going to have a go.

Outside the library, I met the Lord Mayor getting into his car and I told him of my intention. It was quite clear, from the expression on his face that he didn't think much of the idea but, maybe, he also remembered me as the guy who had been trying to influence the direction of his speech inside the library. In any case, he was driven away without further ado. I had to get organised.

It was to be a miso fast. Miso is a soya-based broth and I asked my friends at the Quay Co-op if they would keep me supplied during the fast. It was such an off-the-wall idea that they decided to adopt a hands-off approach and let me sink or swim on my own. I sank, but not until six days had passed.

The local Quakers (I was an Attender, myself) were due to plant a cherry tree near the war memorial at the end of the South Mall, on Hiroshima Day. A small gathering of people convened to mark the occasion and listen to one of the Quaker Elders give a talk.

I had prepared a short written statement for him, outlining my plan for the fast and had it passed to him. I was sitting on the grass, as he started to read it. I paid close attention to him. Feeling that all was going well, I looked away, for a moment and, immediately, he stopped reading my statement and went onto another topic. I felt that my lack of attention had caused this but now, I think it is more likely that he started to see where the statement was leading and decided to pull out, while the going was good.

When the meeting was over, I took up my position, on a bench skirting the footpath. I had a sign, outlining what was going on. As well as fasting from food, I was going to fast from speech and had a notebook and pen, with which to communicate with anyone who wanted to engage with me.

I realised that the cherry tree would die if it didn't get water. I went to Atkins Hardware Store and bought a hose, negotiating the transaction with my notebook and pen, and brought the nose back to the cherry tree, connecting it up to a nearby tap. I turned on the tap and let the water run into the ground adjacent to the tree, and resumed my place on the bench.

There were some young male and female travellers, sitting on the grass behind me. I went over, to make friends with them. One of the young guys grabbed me and judoed me expertly to the ground. I should have beat a hasty retreat, at that point but I was so into a

Jesus head, just then, that I just got up and stood there smiling at him, waiting to see what happened next.

It must have been odd for him, seeing this mute guy, smiling down at him so he threw me again, and again. One of the girls said, "He's queer" and, finally getting the sociology of the situation, I decided that my Peacemaking venture hadn't been a roaring success and went back to my bench.

The word got out that I was fasting for peace and, a couple of nights into the fast, a bunch of people gathered around me on the footpath, and talked and prayed together. I was glad of the company. This unkempt-looking guy came up to me, with a bottle in his hand, and offered it to me. I suspected it was alcohol but also felt that he was asking me to join in his communion so I made a judgement call and took a swig. I knew that I was breaking my fast, but I also knew that I hadn't offended a poor man. However, immediately I gave him back the bottle, one of the ladies present got up and left.

A few nights into the fast, it was cold and there was this middle-aged traveller under a tarpaulin, on the ground behind me. I asked him if I could share his shelter, to get out of the cold. He rolled over and let me in. As soon as I was in, he started to grope me and I got out pronto. This was a communion which wasn't on my agenda.

The following day I was standing on the grass, when this guy grabbed me from behind and thrust his groin into my rear. I was beginning to wonder what was going on in this low-life part of town and what I had got myself into.

The fast was becoming quite painful. I had no support. I was being violated and, most of all, I felt that my family wasn't behind me. So six days after it had begun, I decided to call it off and go home for a meal.

For some reason, I felt that I had to go back to the South Mall, to close the chapter of my fast. It was night-time and I ran into a group of about twenty young gay men, with body language, which was so flexible that I thought they risked losing equilibrium.

Like a seasoned fascist, I told them that they needed to be more erect in their posture and got them to do some spine-straightening exercises, there on the pavement, on the South Mall, at about9.00pm the night I finished my fast. I never saw them again and hope they have forgiven me for my boldness.

By the way: though I had set out for forty and had only reached six, no-one has ever criticised me for it.

An Ominous Instruction
Having tried to stay high since coming back from the Farm, I started to lose altitude and began to enter a black hole in my life. It was as if the sun had disappeared.

One night, walking back home past the Victoria Hospital on Infirmary Road, I had my second 'God

Talks to Declan Directly' episode. This time it was more frightening than previously. Now, God was telling me that He wanted me to kill my Mother. Naturally, I resisted, and quoted the Ten Commandments to support my case. "In that case", said God, "I want you to kill yourself". "OK", I said, with great fear, and headed for the river, at Parnell Place, by the Bus Station. It didn't occur to me that the Ten Commandments prohibited that scenario as much as the previous one.

I was terrified. Under orders from the Supreme Being, with no room for manoeuvre, I jumped into the river but, because protoplasm is lighter than water, floated again with an overwhelming sense of Baptismal energy surrounding me. I saw a small trawler-like boat, moored a little bit downstream from me and thought that it would be suitable for the Farm's Development Organisation, 'PLENTY'.

But I was in no condition to go on a mission for The Farm because I was very shaken, after my experience and decided to seek Sanctuary somewhere safe. The idea of St Stephen's Psychiatric Hospital presented itself to me.

I swam to the nearby steps and, as luck would have it, there was a taxi man, with a taxi, standing at the top of the steps. I could see he was angry and thought it was because I had volunteered for the river. I asked him to take me home, pending a trip to St Stephen's. I wanted to be in from the cold and I could think of no other place to be. He brought me home. I told my folks I was withdrawing for a bit, and we drove to the hospital.

In hospital I was told that I had 'bi-polar disorder' or that I "was bi-polar". It is a sobering experience to be given a handle, which claims to describe your very way of seeing the World, which, in turn, is deemed to be invalid. It's like saying that your whole experience doesn't count and that, unless you take the prescribed dosage of medication you won't be 'well', but that if you do take the prescribed dosage of medication you will be well. I'm not saying that it's invalid to do that, I'm just saying that's how it feels.

There was a doctor in the hospital who was developing a reputation on the teen circuit, for warning them against drugs. I thought that it was ironic that he was telling them to stay away from them while giving them to me.

Teenagers take drugs for hallucinogenic experiences. Our materially based society is dead set against this, because it wants everything tied down. I am not in favour of any synthetic drug but I used to be in love with dope because it is gentle and it is pure and it gets you where you want to go. However I don't take dope anymore because it gets me too high, so each person has to figure it out for themselves. My doctor friend from St Stephen's wouldn't have agreed with this. Neither did he agree when I told him that wanted to leave the hospital, when I felt fine.

He implied that I was weird (not his term) by pointing out that I had cycled naked from Carrigaline and I, in an off-hand sort of way, said, "If it was good enough for Lady Godiva, it's good enough for me" and left him standing there. It wasn't the last I was to hear of this.

I phoned a solicitor friend and, telling him that I was being held at St Stephen's against my will, asked him to write a letter to my doctor friend. The letter arrived and I was released but the doctor decided that he would have the last word and wrote to my solicitor friend finishing the letter with the phrase, "He thinks he's Lady Godiva"

I thought that this was somewhat disingenuous and unprofessional of him but I guess that he knew that I had taken the wind out of his sails and now, he was pulling the carpet from under me.

Grounded

Now that I was on tablets my consciousness was back at Planetary level, for the first time since landing on The Farm. It's interesting to note that Stephen was to tell me later that I had been too high while I had been living there.

3 - Marriage and Africa

In mid-1984 I decided to get married and travel to Africa to work, with my Wife.

The marriage ceremony was held at the Quaker Meeting House in Cork, on September 16 and the celebrations took place in a small hotel outside Midleton, Co. Cork, in the afternoon.

A bunch of musician friends got a band together and entertained our guests for hours. People were to say afterwards, that it had been the best wedding they had ever been at.

Before the wedding, my intended and I had practically no money. A nutritionist friend of ours had suggested that we invite the guests to bring a dish each, to contribute to the wedding feast. This was the strategy we adopted.

We made out a menu and phoned around our guest list, asking them what slot they would like to fill in it. It worked exceedingly successfully The whole wedding cost us £38; a bargain, which I would recommend.

Hindus

One week later we were in Harare, the capital of Zimbabwe, staying with an Indian family in an Indian suburb of the city.

My Wife's friends had offered to put us up until we had found a place of our own. They had also offered to help us find that place, as they had contacts with property-owners in the Indian Community. I felt very grateful for their hospitality and their generosity to us while we were with them. When the time came, they were true to their word and put us in touch with a flat-owner who agreed to let us rent one of his places, in Rotten Row, on the edge of the City-centre.

I had subconsciously assumed, when still in Ireland, that I would be landing in a country of round huts, and peasants working in the fields. Instead I was now living in a socially-stratified, modern city, with a high-rise, reinforced concrete, centre; lush, low-density and medium density residential areas; low-rise apartment blocks and high density suburbs. It appeared to be very well planned, a legacy of UDI where society was colour-coded, but I was told that, since Independence in 1980, there were no colour restrictions on ones place of residence. They were solely economic and, of course the reality of the economy was that the UDI status quo was largely intact, though there was a significant and growing Black Middle Class. We were White Ex-Pats (no reference to our nationality) living on the edge of town in a flat. We had an Indian Landlord, who, though we didn't know it at the time, had plans to eventually get us out and sell the land as it was being rezoned as commercial.

The first night my Wife and I were staying with our Indian Hosts, there was a little intercultural dance, which wasn't entirely comfortable.

In the semi-Hippy culture I had come from, when dinner was over the guest would offer to do the dishes as an expression of gratitude for the meal, and this offer would be accepted as an expression of gratitude for not having to wash up after preparing the meal.

Here in Harare, our hosts had a 'House Boy' who was about twenty two and whose duties included cleaning the house. The Irish equivalent would be a 'Home Help'. This young man lived in a small house in the garden, and was always on duty to wash up after meals.

After our first meal in our Host's house, I did my Irish semi-Hippy thing, and offered to do the dishes. This offer was not well received by the Lady-of-the-House, who let me know, in no uncertain terms, that that particular arrangement was well taken care of. Getting the message, but with mental reservations, I attended to my Ps and Qs, after that.

New Life

The morning of our daughter's arrival dawned and we took a taxi to Umbuya Nehanda Hospital in the area of the Avenue's Clinic.

Umbuya Nehanda was a woman who lived in the early part of the Twentieth Century. She was regarded as a spirit medium and was the inspiration for the First Chimurenga, or Nationalist Uprising, which was put down by the British colonials. It was into the hospital named after this lady, that my Wife was booked to give birth to our baby.

My Wife had kept her own Surname at marriage and
when we got to the check-in desk at the hospital, we
discovered that this was to be a problem. According to
Zimbabwean Law, the baby could only have the
Mother's Surname. My Wife and I had decided that the
baby was to have my Surname and therein lay the
problem.

My Wife's contractions were getting closer and she
wasn't about to hang around debating the point. She
delegated me to deal with it and, with a nurse-midwife,
went off to the Preparation Room. I carried on talking
with the people behind the check-in desk, and
eventually they relented, which is when I joined my
Wife, who was in her final stretch of Labour.

This is where my overweening sense of egalitarianism
got the better of me. There was another woman in the
room. She had been in labour for twenty-four hours and
was having a hard time. I was more aware of this than I
was of the fact that my Wife was having a hard time as
she was better at controlling it.

On a number of occasions, I was at the other side of the
room, comforting the twenty-four-hours-in-labour-
woman, when my Wife needed me at her side. She later
reprimanded me for this. The Birth-Moment was almost
upon and we were taken to the Delivery room. We had
decided that I should catch the baby and had got her
gynaecologist's agreement for this.

Birth is a Sacrament. The nearest technological equivalent, that I can think of, is that of a rocket launch; tens of computers, checking out that millions of systems are 'Go'; de-linking of booms; ignition of fuel, followed by the launch.

Well, our daughter came out, like a rocket and I, positioned, like a scrum-half, gloves on, nearly missed her. But, thank God, I operated reflexively and held her for the first time, realising that she was absolutely conscious. It was a miraculous moment in my life. I can't think why anyone would want to miss it. When our second daughter was born, eighteen months later, it happened at a much slower pace but was equally miraculous and I feel privileged to have been there.

For years I used to proudly tell people how I had 'delivered' my daughters, until one day a woman said to me, "No; your wife delivered your daughters". That took some air out of my balloon, because I realised that I had been kind of assuming that a Woman is designed for childbirth but that I had been breaking new ground.

Of course, for a Woman carrying and giving Birth to a child is a total-involvement thing. This puts my contribution into a perspective which is analogous to the relationship between a Celebrant and an Acolyte (I've been on the Alter and know what it's like when it's Sacramental). We took our baby home.

Before the Birth, my Wife had decided that she wasn't going to spend any more time in the hospital than was

absolutely necessary. She had actually tried to arrange a
Home Birth but had found that the medical
establishment in the City wouldn't support it. For that
reason, after the Birth in hospital, she spent a few hours
in a recuperation room, pending the arrival of our
Indian friends, who were to take us home.

I left her for a half an hour, to fetch a couple of English
friends who were living nearby. As I was walking along
the road, I realised that I was very high and that it was a
very uncomfortable feeling.

In my experience, it is a feature of this state of mind that
one wants everything to be fair and, for this reason,
when our friends arrived and the female partner started
getting very possessive of the baby, and the tea lady
came in and out with cups of tea, I decided that there
was a bit of social position working there, which I didn't
like.

For that reason, when it came time to have the
photograph taken at the hospital door, I gave the baby
to the Tea Lady, and not to our friend.

When the photograph came out, it was clear that our
friend was not very pleased and that I had gone up to a
different level of reality; not an auspicious beginning,
for Fatherhood. We drove home.

When we got home, the Indian Lady took control. This
was highly appropriate. She was the only Lady present,
apart from my Wife, who was still weak from the Birth.
Apart from this, the Indian Lady had two kids of her

own and knew the score. She started to tell me what to fetch, in order to minister to my Wife's needs.

My ego got in the way and I thought that she was treating me as a house boy and told her so.

This was not a good move as she became offended and, with her Husband in tow, walked out the door. Interestingly, he was telling her that I was right. It could have been a gender thing.

In any case, my Wife was in bed with a new-born baby and I was floating around in the outer regions of the Universe and it was not a funny scene. She said she would have been better in hospital but somehow we got through it. But that event must have alerted her to the fact that there were forces at work, which would be very hard to contain.

Our first Material Plane project was to be the building of a nursing seat and, to get some designs, we went to the Library, which was across the road. There, we found a book with a design for a 12.5mm plywood de-mountable seat, which I made and painted red. One of my Wife's students helped with the sanding. At this stage, she was teaching at Prince Edward Boys School, which was a kilometre away.

We registered our daughter's Birth and called her Cáit Rufaro Nomsa. 'Cáit', is the Irish for 'Kate'; 'Rufaro' is the Shona for 'Joy' and 'Nomsa' is the Ndebele for 'As One'. Shona and Ndebele are respectively the majority and minority languages of Zimbabwe.

The Poly

Within a few months of our arrival in Harare, I took up
a position as a lecturer in Harare Polytechnic, known as
'The Poly'. I was to work in the Engineering Department
teaching Maths, Technical Drawing, Management,
Engineering Technology and Building Construction.

I considered this to be a heavy workload but was up-
for-it. A White man ran the Department, which was
mainly staffed by 'Expats', with a few Black junior
members.

In my head, I was tracking at altitude and my language
reflected this. Consequently, my Students often didn't
get the point. In other words, I wasn't a good teacher
because I wasn't delivering at the level of the receiver.

In my first class I gave an enthusiastic delivery on
Independence and the privilege of being able to receive
a Third Level Education. The bolder students let me
know that they had no interest in this stuff and that they
were there to get a certificate and get a job. These guys
were the children of the Revolution and didn't want a
White man coming in and telling them what they knew
already. They simply wanted to get on with it and live
it. So I got on with the class.

When Cáit was born, I told my Class how happy I was
to have assisted at her birth and one guy said, "OK;
you've told us that. Now, can we get on with the class?"

I was experiencing the relativity of age. A few years
later, when I would be teaching at Second Level, I

would have to urge my Students to speak up and ask questions. Obviously, age brings with it greater courage in dealing with authority.

My rarefied classes continued and soon my Deputy Head of Department was brought in to review the situation. He sat in on one of my classes. I delivered, while he watched and, at the end of the class, he took me aside and said that I was using "advanced teaching techniques" and that I should simplify.

I was a bit flattered by his analysis, and sat down while he demonstrated the basic chalk and talk approach. He said he would keep an eye on developments. The next significant development was to be a request to attend a meeting in the Principal's office.

The Picture

In totalitarian countries and countries where there is a Monarch, there is a tendency to have a photograph of the Head-of-State in every public office. It would be possible to write a doctoral thesis on the spiritual, psychological, political and social implications of this practice.

ZANU-PF, the Ruling Party in Zimbabwe, had been taught a few tricks about how to run a country by the North Koreans. This included placing a photograph of Robert Mugabe in virtually every office they could find.

My account of what happened in the Harare Polytech Principal's office is not objective, because the guy sitting next to me didn't see it. But it is what I 'saw', if seeing is believing. And I certainly believed it at the time.

The Principal; my Departmental Head; my Departmental Deputy Head and I were sitting together. The Principal was asking me to explain what was happening in my classes.

I felt that I was under pressure and I noticed that there was a photograph of Robert Mugabe on the wall, overseeing the Principle's desk.

At that time, I regarded Robert Mugabe as a benevolent figure (a position I have long since abandoned), and I wondered how he would feel about what was happening. It seemed to me that if I looked at his photograph, I would pick up clues about his position vis-à-vis the proceedings. The results appeared to be promising. It seemed as if his expression was actually changing as the meeting unfolded.

My Deputy Head looked around to see what I was looking at, and, drawing a blank, gave his attention back to the Principle who was in the process of dismissing me. I left the meeting, went outside, met a bare foot worker, who was cutting the grass, gave him my sandals and walked home.

Some people say that the significance the World has for us is based on our inner thoughts and feelings, a phenomenon called projection. I was projecting my thoughts and feelings onto Robert and he seemed to be sympathising with my position. The other three people, if they were paying any attention to him, were getting a different message and my exit was the result.

This was a very poor performance, indeed. As a kid I had read magazines about alleviating famine in Africa and, for years had nurtured a desire to do something similar when I had grown up. I didn't feel ashamed at being thrown out of The Poly, just puzzled that we didn't see things the same way and, at the same time, having a hard time.

It felt like I was trapped on the top floor of a high-rise building while the foundations were crumbling. My Wife made valiant efforts to tune in to where I was at but she was too grounded for that. She called a priest-friend.

Beitbridge

I started to have auditory hallucinations that a very High Power in the Universe wanted me to travel to Lesotho, to work with a Development Organisation, which I knew was working there. This was very disturbing. After all, Man, I had a Family and couldn't spend my Life, wandering around the World according to the dictates of my high callings. I left for Lesotho.

The first stage of the trip, involved a bus ride to Beitbridge, on the border with South Africa and, on that trip, I sat on the conductor's seat, facing the passengers. I was hallucinating heavily and at one stage, looked at my sandaled feet and they looked like the feet of Jesus. I guess all feet look like that when you are floating high.

We got to Beitbridge and I alighted, immediately getting into a taxi, which was parked at the door of the bus. I felt that my karma was in and then the taxi driver drove me to the Motel. I checked in, then looked around the place.

Arriving in the pool area, I saw a number of neat, White, late-middle-aged gentlemen, on their recliners, reading their newspapers. I felt that this was an unreal situation, in a poor country, and felt that a revolutionary statement was called for. Just to violate the orthodoxy of the situation, I jumped into the pool, in my day cloths, and surfaced to find the situation absolutely unchanged. The gentlemen were still reading their papers and all was calm. End of revolution.

I went to my room and looked in the mirror and saw that I was mad. At that point I chickened out and decided to go home, the following day.

On the following morning, I rose early and, paying for my accommodation, got on the road. Some hours later on the road, I came to a cluster of single-storey buildings, which included a store. I went in and ordered sadza and beans. Sitting outside on the veranda, I looked into the distance. As I ate, a bunch of boys came along and spent a few minutes, jumping up and down in front of me, trying to get into my line of vision. For some reason, I didn't give them the attention they wanted and they left. Then I went to the bus stop.

I can't think why I didn't get the bus in Beitbridge but here I was, now, waiting at a rural bus stop, with a bunch of rural ladies.

I had a bag of nuts and as I talked to the ladies, I offered the nuts around. I could see that one of the ladies was talking about me to the others, then a 'pig' rolled up. A pig is an armoured personnel carrier and in this one was a number of policemen.

The lady agent provocateur went over to the Sergeant and talked to him. He came to me and asked me where I was going and I said, "Harare". He said he would bring me there, which, I thought, was odd, because Harare was hundreds of kilometres away. However, being meek and mild, I went with him and soon we were cruising, at speed, in the back of the pig, on the way to a Police Camp.

On the way to the Police Camp I spoke, mainly to the Sergeant, and we were getting on well. However, periodically, one of his deputies would come over, looking for attention and with a bad attitude. In order to ameliorate the situation I would tell him a joke and he would leave, with a smile on his face.

My other problem was that the co-driver kept coming at me trying to get my passport, which I resisted.

At that point, I wasn't looking at these young men as the legitimate security force so much as a group of uniformed males who had illegitimately lifted me.

At the Police Camp, the co-driver, laughing, got off brandishing my passport and I lunged after him to get it back, landing badly on my shoulder and injuring it. Two young Policemen lifted me up and helped me to the Police Office, where I was installed on a seat, on the front veranda. I didn't know what to do.

They kept me in the office that night and a young officer came in for the night roster. I could see that he was discontent and decided to cheer him up by talking to him. All night I talked to him and the conversation bore results. As the talk rolled on he would periodically toss over one of my possessions: ring, passport and the rest. I realised that I had unintentionally set up an equation between interaction and my stuff.

The following morning, I was back on the front veranda again and, being cosmic, I decided to get telepathic with a friend in Harare, who knew about these things. I felt that the clear signal I was receiving in return, was to run. Which I did.

Heading down the path at speed, away from the Police Office, I had the clear feeling that a bullet was imminently heading in my direction. Instead, two young Police Officers (maybe the previous pair) headed in my direction and, easily catching up with me, grabbed me and brought me back to the office, laughing in a self-congratulatory manner as they did so. I was placed in a cell.

Knowing that this was going to be a hard trip, I found a piece of cotton wool and started to clean the dust off the floor; occupational therapy-in-custody. Soon the interrogation process started, with a stream of officers arriving in sequence at my cell door, and landing me with exactly the same questions.

At that time, in that part of the country there was social unrest and a question of South African involvement. Being White, I was suspect.

Every time I was interrogated I told my interrogator to ring my Wife and gave him the number. Having gone through eight interrogators, none of them did. I decided I would fast.

Three hours into my fast, a group of officers paraded towards the door, one of them, carrying a tray with a cotton towel draped over it. They were obviously bringing me a meal. I told them that I was fasting and they were really offended because they started showering rocks through the grill in the cell-door. I sat with my back to the wall, watching the rocks hitting the wall opposite me. Soon the officers left but my fast may have made a difference because the next interrogator to come to me looked more intelligent and compassionate than the previous ones, and rang my Wife when I asked him.

I knew this because, the following morning, I was called to the Camp Superintendent's house and offered tea and the news that I would be travelling, by the next bus, to

Harare under the supervision of the driver. Where the authority structure is lean, functions have to be exercised with flexibility. I was to be met in Harare by the local Police. The police weren't there when we got to Harare.

When I arrived in Harare my Wife met me at the bus, and told me that she had realised that she could live by herself. We went home.

Unitarian

Through going to the Quaker Meeting every Sunday, we had met a Unitarian priest, called Fr Ted, who was very mature and grounded and my Wife and he had connected. She asked him to help.

Though I was getting flakier and flakier, I felt I was under scrutiny but didn't know what to do about it. I knew that I was experiencing a different reality but didn't want to give it up because, though it was hard, it was hugely interesting. That is why, the first time Fr Ted said he would pick me up for hospital, I absconded. But eventually, my Wife persuaded me to go and I went. She checked me into the Annex of Parirenatwa Hospital.

The first day I was there we were out in the courtyard and it felt to me that the 'atmosphere' was very stiff and tight. It felt that my head was set in a dense jelly and that, if I moved, something outside myself would rupture. I was picking up on the fact that no one around me was moving; everyone was absolutely still and I was uncomfortable about causing a ripple. I started picking up leaves, to stay sane.

'Under observation' is a term, which corresponds to real conditions. In the Annex, we patients roved in the day-room or the courtyard while the nurses sat behind a grill doing their knitting and, presumably, glancing up at us, from time-to-time. I can't comment on its therapeutic value.

While in hospital, I took up smoking again after a four-year abstinence.

Daily, my Wife brought me veggie burgers, which she had made and transported in a food flask. My birthday came.

On the day of my birthday, my Wife arrived to accompany me home but, before the doctor would give his agreement, he required me to do a test. The test involved drawing, on a simple map, the most effective route between two points.

My Wife was anxious that I wouldn't buck the system by refusing to do the test, and urged me to do so. I drew a line on the piece of paper and we left for the birthday meal. Soon after, I was released from the Annex. I was back at home and on heavy medication. I hadn't got a job and spent my days at home, miserable and lying on the bed, while my Wife went out to work.

This is the thing with Bi-Polar, the medication is critical. Too little, and you go up; too much and you go down. I was way down and didn't have the smarts to have my medication reviewed as I thought it was my own responsibility to get well, by sheer will.

Terence

Cáit was growing. At her first Birthday Party, she nearly stood on her cake, which, at that moment was on the living room floor. Luckily, at the last instant, she was whisked away by my attentive Wife.

During this renewed period of unemployment, I used to take Cáit to visit our neighbours, Terence and his Sarah. They were both elderly and were unusual, because he was White and she was Black. They had lived their Marriage through a time when he would have been shunned by White colleagues and friends because of their liaison.

They were very hospitable to us and we always enjoyed our visits. A couple of years later, Terence died and I wept. My friends and I organised the funeral.

Terence and I had a common trait; we used to go 'walkabout'. He had Parkinson's disease and was on heavy medication. Regularly he would take off on walks and continue walking until his legs gave out and he dropped; then he would be taken home in a scarred state. He had a kind heart and I loved the times our toddler and I spent with him and Sarah. I hope he is going walkabout in a safer place.

Bulawayo

The Ministry for Labour, which ran the Poly, was still paying me but I had no job. I heard they were short-staffed in Bulawayo Poly. I contacted their Head of Civil Engineering and went to see him. He turned out to be a very pleasant man and my pleasure at our meeting was heightened by the fact that he offered me a job. I located a house and returned home, with both a house and a job lined up.

My Wife and I planned our departure, deciding that part of that plan would be a party for our friends the Saturday night before the Monday on which we were due to leave.

We had the party, and the truck we had booked arrived on Monday morning to pick up our stuff. Out of courtesy, I called to the Director at the Ministry for Labour to tell him that Bulawayo Poly had engaged me, and that I was leaving Harare. He said that he hadn't been consulted on the appointment, and that he wouldn't be sanctioning it. With an ashen face and my tail between my legs I made my way back to my Wife who was supervising the loading of the truck.

I wasn't pleased with the Director because he was depriving me of a job and depriving Bulawayo Poly of a lecturer, on the basis that the Head of Department wasn't authorised to recruit staff, even at a time of shortage. Of course, the Head of Department could have informed the Director. It was Post-Independence Zimbabwe - maybe all the lines of demarcation hadn't been worked out. In any case, I had to tell my Wife to ask the workers to offload the truck and replace our stuff in the flat, which they did, charging us nothing at all for their total service. I had witnessed tightness and generosity in the same morning.

At this stage, we were employing a Lady to look after our daughter. One day, my Wife came home and announced that she had got me a job at her School, teaching Maths, Physics and General Science. She brought me to meet the Principal. My classes started and I felt much better, as I had something in which to engage my mind. I was up and running.

The Non-Aligned Summit

Our flat, on Rotten Row, was facing the Harare Sheraton Hotel. Yugoslav workers had recently built the hotel, as a gift from Yugoslavia to Zimbabwe. My Wife and I had been attending meetings of ZONE, the Zimbabwe Organisation for Nuclear Education. I had become concerned about the potential South African nuclear threat and would, subsequently, organise a public meeting on the subject.

The research I had done had told me that South Africa probably had the potential to deliver nuclear weapons into Zimbabwe and surrounding countries and that their weapons programme was at an advanced stage. I was surprised that there was no public discussion on this topic.

The Harare Sheraton had been chosen as the venue for the Non-Aligned Movement's Summit and, as well as the participants, hundreds of journalists were due to attend. We put a "Welcome" sign, on our balcony and a Council official told us to take it down. We rang the Town Clerk and he said to ignore the official.

The Summit commenced and I decided that I was going to talk to journalists about the SA nuclear threat; but how to get into the Summit? There was a drive into the Hotel and it was blocked by two checkpoints. There was a lady ahead of me walking towards the first checkpoint and I caught up with her. I saw that she had an ID and got into conversation with her. In the back of my mind, I knew that I might be compromising her security clearance but, so concerned was I about the possibility of the annihilation of Zimbabwe, that I let that thought pass. The guys at the security points merely glanced at us and let us through.

Now I was standing in a courtyard, at the back of the Hotel, and through a door in front of me was the assembly hall for the journalists. I approached the door and, trying as hard as I could to look like a journalist, walked past the security guy at the desk. He showed no reaction; I did. So surprised was I that he had let me through, I looked back at him, as if to say, "You mean it's all right?" He told me to step outside, so I returned to the courtyard and got into conversation with a few journalists, one from the United States.

I told them why I was at the Summit and the American journalist kept saying, "You're kidding!" as if he didn't believe what I was saying. Before I could sort that one out we were approached by a group of Black men in suits, wearing sun glasses, who politely dismissed the journalists and took me by the wrist to the nearby security building.

I was run through identical batteries of questions by a retinue of interrogators whose main concern was how I had got in. They were the guys who had put the check points and ID system in place and they were finding it hard to accept that their system had been breached.

Their next move was to take me to my flat, to check my address, and when my Wife saw that I was in custody, she gave me a royal bollocking, in front of my captors. This entertained them no end and I could feel my warrior mantle slipping a notch or two.

Next stop was Harare Police Station, where they took me to a room and eight guys started throwing questions at me. While they were obviously enjoying the process the underlying purpose was to wear me down and find inconsistencies in my story. On reflection, I had been trying to raise awareness about the possibility that their country could be attacked from the south and they were running me through a cat and mouse routine. I didn't get the impression that they were interested in the content of my story. One guy asked me if I had ever been in hospital.

I lied and said I had visited them and the questioning continued. Then in came my Wife and two friends, and one friend said that I had been in hospital, at which point my captors laughed and let me free. I told my liberators, in the car park, that I hadn't appreciated their intervention. It was like saying, "This guy is nuts; there is no potential nuclear threat from South Africa; he didn't breach your security; nothing happened; nothing will happen; let's forget the whole thing and all go home"

School

The School was a former 'A' School, Whites only, but since Independence had been open to kids of all Races and now had an almost totally Black enrolment, with some Indian and White boys as well.

The School, situated on about five hectares of immaculately-kept grounds, was run by a former Rhodes Scholar who ran a very tight and disciplined ship. There were over one thousand Students.

I started three choirs, a rowing team and set a brass ensemble in motion. Our senior choir won their section at the Annual Eisteddfod; our Fours won their race at the Annual Regatta at Mazoe Dam; and the Ensemble played at the Annual School Concert, which I organised. Every day, I walked from class to class saying "Good morning" to everyone I met – School policy - and the boys would raise their hats, in return, saying, "Good morning, Sir". I met no discipline problems.

On the extra-curricular side, I was doing very well and my classes were also progressing well, especially with the A-Level Physics Class.

However, I had an encounter with my Science Head of Department when he gave me a broadside, having inspected my 2B5 Class's Science notes.

I had concentrated on teaching them, using exposition and questions to put the material across. I didn't spend sufficient time writing notes on the board because I was treating them as if they had the skills of University students, who could take it down as the class unfolded. This is what my Head of Department spotted.

With the deep resonance of a large-framed Afrikaner, he condemned my effort and told me that I was putting the boys' educational future at risk. I could see that he cared deeply for those boys but had the distinct feeling that he was enjoying the process of denunciation. He was the man who had told me on a previous occasion, that he knew Nelson Mandela personally, and that Nelson wasn't all that he was cracked up to be. Is it a good idea to go around putting doubts in peoples' minds about people who are holding it together, for all of us?

Ironically, the week before my encounter with my HoD, his Deputy had inspected my class to review my teaching, and had given me a glowing report because all my students were answering the questions correctly. I had them engaged and running with it, but the records were sparse.

The Clinic

Eighteen months after Cáit was born my Wife and I went to The Avenues Clinic for the Birth of our second daughter, who would be called Aoife, later abbreviated to Leaf. On the way, we stopped off at friends to deposit Cáit and stayed for tea. Consequently by the time our taxi reached the entrance to The Clinic, my Wife was in the final stages of labour, so I went in and brought out an attendant pushing a wheelchair. He wheeled her to the Labour Room, while I attended to the paperwork.

It was a quick Birth; she pushed; I caught and we were a four-person Family.

Back At School

Another class I was given, was the 2B11 Class. These boys had one response, which they used constantly. Every time I made a statement they said, "Why?" When I attempted to explain my previous statement, they repeated "Why?" It didn't take me long to realise that their game was to let me do all the running while they stood still, on a monosyllable. I decided that they weren't interested in the curriculum and started giving them mathematical games to play with. They were interested in this. I decided to go to the principal to discuss what I had found and what I was doing.

He was adamant that that the 2B11 boys would study the curriculum; it was non-negotiable. I felt my heart sink. I didn't want to face a year of "Whys" from boys who were only interested in using that question to avoid learning. Also, I knew I could get these guys interested in other stuff which would be good for their minds and which would also provide them with some legitimate entertainment. It was not to be.

As the guy who was in charge of choirs, I had handed over the Juniors to a teacher from Canada who wanted them to sing a song in praise of the original patron of the school. I took the position that our students' parents wouldn't like their sons singing the praises of a colonial overlord and decided to find out what the staff felt. Half the Blacks were in favour; all the White Zimbabweans were against and all the White expats were against. I brought the matter to the principal. He said to me that he recognised the sensitivity of the situation but it was obvious to me that he was unwilling to do anything about it. In the middle of this, the teacher from Canada resigned as conductor of the choir. She subsequently resumed her position but I wasn't tracking the situation sufficiently carefully to know if her original plans stood.

There was a White teacher in the School who was a bully and used to cane the boys, though it was against School policy; the practice was that only the Principle caned.

Stephen once said that he came to a point in his life, where he realised he was attached to things turning out fair. He also used to teach about neither giving nor taking social position.

This was kind of where I was at as I was walking past this teacher's class one day and I saw him caning a student. I walked in and told the class that he shouldn't be doing that, when he grabbed me and propelled me out the door, at speed.

I wasn't prepared for that and, gathering myself together debated whether I should go to the Principle. But I felt that this was the sort of thing that happened to me when I got high and decided to let it go lest it blow further up in my face.

I don't like some of the vocabulary around turning ourselves on. It reminds me of limiting words, like 'schizophrenia', a pejorative term which demeans people.

My generation was programmed to believe that turning yourself on was the key to hell and it is well known that belief can be a self-fulfilling prophecy. My belief sent me to Hell many times in my teens, and while in the School I didn't want any of my students experiencing that agony. One day in class, I gave my students the Golden Rule: "Don't agonise about it; do it and forget about it". At the end of the Year I received a letter from the Principle, saying that he would not be renewing my contract. I thought of my Golden Rule and felt that the letter was the Institutional response.

Of course, there may have been no cause-effect relationship between those two events but the letter caused me to wonder about the relationship between compassion, honesty and propriety. I was out of a job again.

Actions on First Street

During our seven-year stay in Zimbabwe, I helped organise a number of events at the corner of First Street and Union Avenue. This was a pedestrianised part of town. These were all consciousness-raising events and made no contribution to the GDP of the country or raised the living standards of the rural poor.

ZONE wanted to commemorate Hiroshima Day and came up with the idea of a 'Die In' where a group of people would lie on the ground for a few minutes, be photographed by the media and hand out Press Releases.

It was necessary to get police permission for this event and due to their uncertainty about what to expect, they sent a riot squad to cover it.

So on the day, there were about one hundred participants and about as many bored-looking riot police giving the impression they wished they were somewhere else.

The following year, the message had got through; "ZONE is peaceful", so they let us alone when we staged a play, put on by students from the University of Zimbabwe

The third event of which I was a part was on a United Nations Day of Solidarity with South African Political Prisoners. For this, I designed metal cages, had them fabricated at a local engineering shop and erected in downtown Harare. The event was opened by the

Speaker of the House, standing on a sewing box which I had made for my Wife (he subsequently fell from grace), and a bunch of young people and I spent the night in the cages, learning what it feels like to be political prisoners.

The Irish Connection

Soon after we arrived in Harare, I realised that there had been a strong Irish connection to the City in colonial and UDI times, with a lot of Irish place names dotted around the city. This was also true of the business life of Harare. I was to work with one such company.

Walking along the street one day, I saw two White guys ahead of me, walking in the same direction. By the way he walked, I just knew that one of them was Irish and ran to catch up with them, introducing myself when I reached them. They told me that they were quantity surveyors working as part of an Irish triangular team, producing designs for government contracts.

When I told them I was an engineer, they told me that Nicholas O'Dwyer and Partners, part of their team, was looking for engineers. I decided to go and see NOD.

I met the managing director and he said he would take me on and promised special treatment, because I was Irish. This irritated me, because I didn't want special treatment. Because his company was designing barracks for the army, I told him that I would work only on civilian contracts. He agreed to that and I started work.

I was given three contracts: The Murewa Drainage scheme, The ZESA Training Centre, and The Government Curriculum Development Unit.

Murewa was a 'Growth Point', which is to say, it had been set aside for special development and was one of many around the country, which had been thus designated after Independence. One of the changes that had been made in creating the growth points was around land tenure. Unlike the situation in the rest of the Rural Areas, where land was vested in the President and administered by the chiefs, people running businesses in the Growth Points could own their own sites. This measure was deemed necessary to attract business to the GPs. The project I was involved on incorporated the design of a buried drainage system for Murewa, which was the size of a small village. I didn't enjoy this project because I had misgivings about designing a system which would require so much water, in an area where water was scarce. I don't know if it went ahead as I had left NOD beforehand.

My second project was the oversight of the Civil Works on a large training centre which was being constructed for the Zimbabwe Electricity Supply Authority, by a British Engineering Company. This work involved visiting the site a couple of times a week, reviewing progress and reporting to the MD.

The government were about to introduce their own second level curriculum and, in order to do so, had commissioned the design of a Unit where the new curriculum would be developed, to replace the British O and A levels. While I was at NOD I oversaw the Civil Works, on behalf of the Client.

However, I was not happy at NOD. Mine was a square job, with a company which had ties to the military. I did my work effectively and, when two of my projects were complete the MD let me go, because I wasn't buying into the company ethos or the esprit de corps, which he liked to encourage.

Rebuilt

There was an explosion at a block of flats, half way between our flat and the School. The explosion happened in the flat of an ANC official who was living there with his wife. She died in the explosion. Their flat was ruined by the blast and nearby flats suffered as well. The partial ruin laid there for months, a testimony to the belief in chaos-as-the-road-to-salvation.

The day after the explosion, I was walking in the direction of the flats when I saw a roadblock manned by a policeman and a soldier in front of me. The roadblock was on the street, so I kept walking on the footpath, though I knew, in my heart, that I was violating the rules. Because of where my head was at, I didn't want to be interrupted by any State arrangements.

As I was walking along the footpath, the soldier disrespectfully hissed at me and demanded to know where I was going. Uncharacteristically, I lied to him and said that I was a Citizen of the country, and didn't have to tell him anything about myself. Then I walked across the road, towards a nearby School-Playing-Field, and I heard him cock his gun. My legs turned to jelly, but I kept going. He didn't shoot.

This event demonstrates how, in my elevated state of mind, I was denying the institutional and physical realities in my vicinity, thereby putting myself in danger. Ultimately I was saved by the humanity of that soldier, who decided he wasn't going to shoot me in the back. However, I was tracking at a different level as well.

I felt that we should do something about the flats, as it was a bad message to have them lying there, in a ruined state. Jenny, at the Quakers, spoke to me one Sunday about it and I realised that we were in accord. I decided to go into action and my Wife and I organised a meeting at our flat for interested people. The meeting decided that we were going to go for it and rebuild the flats.

We read that a Church political group had decided the same thing and met them to form an alliance, out of which the Heal The Wounds Campaign was born.

I was the first co-ordinator and recruited six young people to work on the initial phase of fund-raising, which was when my Wife had a brainwave.

The flats were insured but the insurance money wouldn't be enough to engage a conventional contractor to rebuild them. However, she knew a contractor who was prepared to work on a labour-only basis, provided the Campaign supplied plant and materials. Because we would be able to avoid overheads, it turned out that the insurance money would be enough. The work went ahead. I acted as resident engineer, and on completion the flats were reoccupied.

While the Campaign was rebuilding the flats we realised that South African-sponsored bandits, from Mozambique, were attacking people along the eastern border of the country. These bandits were known as the MNR or Renamo.

A local pastor and I made a trip to the eastern districts to find out what was happening. In a tea estate we met a group of young men who had had their ears chopped by the bandits. Holding back my tears I felt a sense of utter hopelessness at the thought that we were supposed to do something about this. Further on, in a Mission Hospital we met people whose skulls had been open. We were inspired by the staff, who sang and danced in the wards to keep their patients spirits up. Returning to Harare, I wrote a report upon which the Campaign's further strategy was to be based.

By this time, I was working with a Rural Development Organisation, in a provincial capital, in the East of the country, travelling home at weekends to spend time with my Family. By now we were living as Wardens at the Quaker Meeting House, in Lincoln Green, outside Harare. I liked this name, because I kind of identified with Robin Hood.

Rural Development

The organisation I worked for was set up as its development wing, by a national Church Body. It had its Head Quarters in Harare and was funded by donations from the German Church, who vetted all its programmes. The office I arrived in, as water engineer, was responsible for projects in two Provinces. I was cruising high when I landed there and was soon to have two run-ins with the National Chairman and the Local Chairman.

A National Training Day had been called and the National Chairman was due to address the opening session. He started by saying that the thing that most characterised Jesus was the way he drove the traders out of the Temple. I don't know what he had in mind but, to me, at that moment, he was setting us up for a critical rant and I said to him that Jesus' over-riding characteristic was his compassion.

This set the cat among the pigeons and he demanded to know who I was and roared at me that he was my employer. I remained quiet and the meeting continued.

What I wasn't allowing for was the fact that he had the floor, he was the National Chairman. Acting on a voluntary basis and in Zimbabwean Society, one didn't challenge authority. Bad move. I was to pay for it.

At around the same time, back in the Provinces, the local Chairman asked me to drop him and his potatoes home, in one of the organisation's trucks. I agreed. His home was some distance away. We got to the entrance to his land and the truck was now moving along a deeply furrowed track, which I deemed to be a danger to our suspension.

When we got to the Chairman's house, I gave him a little lecture about endangering organisation property. I am sure he didn't appreciate being lectured to, by this Murungu (White man), from Ireland and he, pointedly, asked me if I valued my job. I got the point and dropped it; he didn't, as time would prove.

A female friend was due to visit me with her kids, in the Provincial Capital, and when I got on her bus I welcomed all the people in it. She was really pissed off at being publicly humiliated, as she saw it.

A Russian Football Team had just arrived in a local Hotel and I wanted to welcome them. I went in and addressed them about how delighted I was with the introduction of Glasnost and Perestroika. They looked embarrassed, so I left.

There has been a lot of talk in recent years, about 'social space' and 'personal space'. My experience of these phenomena, is that in the early stages of being high, one is acutely aware of them and can function very successfully in human situations. However, as one's altitude increases, the demarcation lines disappear and one is up in everyone's space, because their energy is so attractive.

Everyone loves to be up in babies' energy because they are so Holy and juicy (to use a term out of the Hippy movement), and babies' social space can be very small. You can be up in an Adult's space, with love in your heart and she will recoil because you are giving her more energy and attention than she wants. But it is socially and culturally variable; some people don't want you less than three feet away from them; others can handle six inches; it's a matter of preference.

On the work front, things were going well. Our team, run by a very competent Foreman, was setting up base in one of our two Provinces-of-responsibility. It soon became obvious to me that my role would be a support-role, ensuring that equipment and materials were delivered on time.

There was a guy working in the office, handling the mail, and he lived in a little eight foot by four foot room in the garden behind the office. He had no light, in his room, and I said, "Bad teaching", and it was fixed.

Our projects consisted of digging wells or drilling boreholes in rural villages, where previously, the women had to walk kilometres to the nearest clean stream or water hole. The deal was that we would build a fence around the pump when the job was done. Then the local ladies would lay stones' in the enclosure, to ensure firmness underfoot.

This day, a Delegation from Head Office and the Provincial Office came to visit one of our projects. It was raining. The ladies of the village were laying stones in the enclosure and when they saw the Delegation they started dancing to express their gratitude. My heart broke and I danced with them, while the delegation looked on. I didn't know if I was violating social protocol but felt that a bit of solidarity was in order.

On the same tour, I got to another village ahead of the delegation. I started clowning around and had the people of the village rolling and chortling. The delegation arrived and handshakes were exchanged. Such was the come-on of the delegation that the villagers immediately wiped the smiles off their faces and metamorphosed into mourners, at their own funeral.

The National Vice Chairman was due to visit a well and the guy who was putting up the fence asked me to negotiate with the VC as he was getting only seventy zim dollars per week; less than the minimum wage. I did this when the VC arrived, but was told that the rate was set by the donor. Negotiating in front of the fence erecting guy was not a good idea according to local usage, and didn't help my tenure.

We had a Dynamiser. She was the Lady who would go into villages, in advance of an installation, and negotiate with the villagers on timing, position and so on. She told me that the pump always finished up near the chief's house. I didn't get into that issue.

We needed concrete for one of our projects and I went to Harare, to negotiate with the only supplier in the country and brought the kids with me, dropping into the Head Office on the way. We got the concrete but I got a rap on the knuckles in my assessment, for bringing the kids to work. I was overestimating the revolutionary state of the organisation.

The work continued and our teams installed loads of pumps around the Provinces. I continued to suggest ways in which we could improve things, as I was always looking to the future and this irritated the Co-ordinator, who was a fine Lady. She had been born on a Mission and, one day, she told me that that made her a 'Mish Kid'.

To introduce a bit of popular physics here: Einstein introduced the idea of Time, as the Fourth Dimension. It is easy to assume that we are all in the same place on that dimension. It is my belief that we are spread along it, in a Bell Curve of Distribution; meaning, we are not all in the same place, time-wise.

People who are high, tend to live in the future and, consequently, tend to see the shortcomings in present arrangements. This can be a valuable function if it maintains continuity with present arrangements and is prepared to live with them. However, my Co-ordinator felt that she was putting in too much time 'counselling' me and that I wasn't sufficiently grounded in the present. As a result of this I was discharged at the end of my probation. I was given a week's notice but left immediately, travelling to Harare by bus.

The Street People

Arriving by bus, back in Harare where my Family lived, I alighted outside the Railway Station. There were about one hundred homeless people there; either talking in groups or cooking over open fires.

I felt called to be involved with these people and I went over to one group and introduced myself. I was offered a cup of tea, a tin drum to sit on, and the conversation started. I asked my hosts why they were there and they said:

·No job

·Fleeing the war, in the Rural Areas and never going back

·Being put out of their houses by unsympathetic stepmothers

Through a process of discussion, we decided that we needed to set up an organisation, build on the skills that were there and get viable. They said that they would do a community survey and I said I would come back the following day, to see how things were going.

The kids were growing up, with a lovely garden to play in. I may have been a lousy Husband but I was a wonderful Father, because I was able to tune into the magic consciousness, which is characteristic of kids. Now that I was back in Harare full time, I would be spending far more time with them and enjoying lots of outings.

The following day, I returned to the Street People with my guitar, sang a few inspirational songs to raise energy, and the meeting started. They told me there were twenty ladies in the Community who could raise chickens. We knew that raising chickens was a low-income activity, but, in the absence of any alternative, decided that we would go for it and start a Co-op.

The government was interested in fostering co-ops but, as we were to find out, a chicken-raising co-op was not going to be possible, because we had no land.

Later, on the day of the meeting, a reporter from a national newspaper interviewed a few members of the Organisation and they told him that they were going to start a chicken-raising operation. The report was published the following morning and, that evening police came, burned property and moved everyone on. There were about thirty kids in the group.

One kilometre along the main road, there was a piece of open land and the urban refugees landed there and set up base. They were now squatters, though for the next year and a half, they retained the name 'Street people'.

Half the people foraged plastic and wood and erected 'igloos'; the remaining plastic was provided by a pastor from the Dutch Reformed Church and, so, all the people were sheltered.

A few of the young leaders of the community and I
visited the Department of Agriculture and told them
that we would like training in chicken raising, because
we wanted to start a co-op. They said that, in order to
get training, we would have to register with the
Department of Co-ops first. So we went there. They said
that they wouldn't register us as a co-op until we had
land, which we could get by writing to the Municipality.

We wrote to the Municipality, but never received a
reply to our request. Due to lack of motivation and
devotion to bare survival, SPO didn't follow up the
chicken raising option and the idea died.

Our next project was sanitation. Some of the young men
dug two latrines and erected enclosures. The latrines
were soon filled, due to the numbers on the site.

I suggested that there be elections for a committee and
these were held, resulting in a group of six, which met
every Saturday. Some people, who hadn't been elected,
used to turn up at the meetings and I mentioned this.
No-one took me up on it and I assumed it was accepted.
I dropped the subject.

There were about thirty children in the community, and
I put it to the committee that we needed a school.
Within a week, one of the Elders had built a small
school of thatch, and in an act of synchronicity, two
young Jewish Women just out of school, arrived from
England and became our teachers. The school continued
meeting for a year-and-a-half and was our success story.

There was a tap across the road from the site and some of the young men got a hose and hooked it up; thereby providing water for the community.

I was spending a lot of time with the Street People, but I wasn't putting any food on the table. I reasoned that, since my Wife had a job, the Family would be looked after and I was free to pursue my human rights work. The flaw in my reasoning was that I didn't have my Wife's agreement for this.

PAC

The freedom struggle was continuing in South Africa – Azania - and one day an elderly representative of the PAC, Pan Africanist Congress of Azania, stood on a box, in First Street and made a speech. He said that he wanted money to buy guns, to overthrow the white apartheid regime in his country. If I had been a Buddhist, I probably would have moved on, but being a kind of gung-ho non-violent activist, I started to heckle him and my vibes were so bad that he fell off his box. That was the end of the meeting but one of his security guys came over to me and took me, by the wrist, to the speaker. Realising that I had hurt the feelings of this old man I apologised and was released.

The Street People, Continued

We were trying to build a basic community, which had little energy and less skill, except for the skill of surviving out of trash bins and foraging for firewood. The community continued to meet on Saturdays and the whole community met on Sunday morning to discuss the decisions the committee had come to the day before. It had the effect of consolidation of identity.

Two Church groups offered training in dressmaking and carpentry for some of the women and men, but the carpentry offer wasn't taken up because the men were too sick to travel the long distance involved.

SPO was building community identity, educating the kids, but was not providing food for its people.

An Evangelical Church group, whom I had previously approached for sponsorship, came on site. When I had asked the group leader to sponsor me, he had asked me if I was "born again". I had replied, "Every day" and he had said that he would consider sponsoring me if SPO got a Constitution together. While we were doing that, his Church made a direct approach to the people.

They said that if the people allowed them to hold religious services, on site, they would be prepared to give food to those who attended.

The committee discussed this proposition at our Saturday meeting, and I was uneasy about it. However, there was no arguing with food and it was decided to let the Evangelicals hold their Sunday meetings. It started off pretty low-key, but pretty soon it became clear that they wanted to turn the community into a Church and that they saw the SPO as an impediment in their plan. We were a representative democracy and they were a hierarchical system. They started bad mouthing SPO as doing the devil's work.

This broke my heart, but SPO continued running the school; started a football team and a netball team; and liaised with the police public relations dept. This bore no fruit as the police started to pick up every derelict person in the city and drop them off at the site. At one stage we had fifty, which was a bit of a load, considering the general energy level of the group.

So, there were two levels of authority running in parallel; one, top-down; one horizontal; and they weren't communicating. It was if they were competing for the souls of the people. Another Church offered to help and set up its own committee. I told them that SPO had its own structures and invited them to work through that. They declined and withdrew their offer.

On the first anniversary of SPO's founding, a celebration was held and folks from various NGOs came and joined us for food and entertainment. The entertainment included a football game between SPO's team and a team from my old school. SPO won but I was grateful that my old head had sufficient social mobility to send his team along.

I was in the habit of saying, "We", when referring to SPO and a lady from a local NGO took exception to this. It caused a huge rift between us and is indicative of the power of words; in a negative or positive direction.

We weren't paying sufficient attention to hygiene, and rats appeared on the site. I went to the chief medical officer for the city and asked him to send in his rodent control squad. In a menacing fashion, he said he would see to it that the people were burned out and I left his office, wondering how someone who should be committed to human health and well being could have such a threatening attitude.

This meeting sent warning bells through my mind and I wrote to Robert Mugabe offering to look after the lost sheep while he looked after the main flock. Apart from the fact that I wasn't looking after the lost sheep very well, this letter (if he saw it) may have alerted Robert to the fact that there were squatters at the site.

No Visa

I had been in the country for six years and had no Visa. I was an illegal immigrant. I wasn't happy with this and decided to do something about it. Apart from having been kicked out of a number of employments, my record of service to the country was pretty good and so I wrote to the Speaker to the House of Representatives, to whom I was known, seeking amnesty.

In reply, I received a letter telling me to report to the Minister for Home Affairs, which I did. The Minister showed me into his office and gave me a little talk about loyalty to the leadership, which I felt was an attempt to silence me. To disagree would have meant no Visa; to agree would have meant capitulation so I remained silent. It was an uncomfortable encounter.

However, the outcome was satisfactory. Within a few days I received a letter, saying that my application had been successful and that, in a few weeks, I could pick up my Visa at the Visa Office.

Burnt Out

The Minister for Education took an interest in our school and asked to see some of our people. On the morning of the appointed meeting, a large number of gun-carrying soldiers and police with dogs entered the site and arrested all the people, including thirty children, and then, torched all the shelters, burning the people's belongings. They then brought everyone to Central Police Station.

One of the community escaped and phoned me. I cycled to the site, met him and one of our teachers as well. All that was left were the burnt-out shelters. We decided to keep our appointment with the Minister for Education and walked to her office. I told her that her government had burnt out our village and she remained quite impassive. She was more interested in why my male comrade was sleeping rough, when he had A levels.

I could have ranted at her and demanded to know why ZANU-PF was attacking its own people – including babies and children but the situation was so surreal and she probably hadn't ordered the attack anyway, that we had this very civilised meeting while our people were in cells in Central Police Station.

The three of us returned to the site and saw trucks passing, carrying our people. We loaded into the teacher's car and following them, then realised that they

were on their way to a high security prison outside
town. The irony of this was heightened by the fact that
this prison had housed ZANU-PF cadres during UDI.

The three of us went to the Meeting House and called
every journalist we could think of and invited them to a
Press Conference on the site, the following day. One of
the journalists apparently called police public relations
for a comment, because while we were calling more
journalists, the police public relations officer,
accompanied by two high-ranking officers, arrived at
the door.

The PRO asked me to call off the Press Conference and I
said that because he hadn't kept his promise to keep us
informed on police plans we would go ahead with it.
The Press Conference was held the following day.

About ten journalists turned up and, among them was
one from South African Radio. I was so PC in those days
that I didn't want our disaster giving succour to the
apartheid regime and told him that I didn't want him at
the Press Conference. He was a professional and wasn't
going to be put off by this, but he was good enough to
offer me the opportunity of listening to his report the
following day, at a café in town which he nominated. I
accepted and the Press Conference went ahead. I met
him the following day and told him that his report was
an excellent one. He said I had guts and we parted
friends. The Press Conference got wide coverage in all
but the government papers.

Two days later, having been 'assessed' by a team of social workers, our people were released from prison and walked back to the site. The police had put out the word that no one was to occupy it and so there was a problem. I said that I would bring the ladies and the children to the Quaker Meeting House (without the agreement of the Quakers), and the men scattered to where they wouldn't be found. We found transport for the ladies and the children and a local pastor drove me, behind them. He said he would open his Church Hall to all the people the following day.

I showed the ladies the toilets but they were unaccustomed to using them and used the garden instead. This led to domestic disharmony.

The following day, we had a meeting on the site and a police superintendent was present, to see that no one stayed. There was a team from national television there also. I started to speak to tell the folks that we were leaving the site and moving to the pastor's Church Hall, when the cameraman put his camera about six inches from my face and threw me off completely. Mine was not a good delivery.

One of our guys started up a ritual denunciation of the government and the camera turned to him. That was what was carried on television that night, which surprised me, given that the Station was government-controlled.

The people landed in the Church Hall and the
Evangelicals came and distributed clothes. The Elders of
the Church decided to have a meeting to discuss the
situation. After the meeting they told the people that
they were being offered a place outside town, with jobs,
and everyone loaded into trucks to get there. 'There'
was the farm of one of the Elders.

It broke my heart to see the way the people scrambled
into the trucks, paying no attention to each other and
landing on top of each other but, I guess, the niceties of
human behaviour get lost when survival is at stake.

When the people landed at the farm, they were given a
large, empty house to stay in and they laid out the
bedding they had left. There was a small church next to
the house and we discovered that the land, occupied by
the house and the church, was owned by the Catholic
Church. The farmer had put the people there, adjacent
to his land, without the agreement of the RC Church
and he was going to see the bishop after the weekend, to
explain matters.

When the farmer met the bishop, the bishop explained
to him that the RC Church wanted the house for
training priests, which put the farmer in a pickle.
Ironically the bishop put the matter in the hands of his
Justice and Peace Commission, for a speedy resolution.
Meanwhile the community settled in and an NGO
supplied enough food for a communal kitchen to be set
up. One of the teachers came every day, and ran the
school.

In the absence of a latrine the people used the land surrounding the house. There was so little energy in the community that, when I tried to muster a few folks to dig one, no one responded. These people were wasted after living for years on the streets, on a piece of land and in prison. The farmer offered work to a small number of people but he wasn't satisfied with their performance.

The Evangelicals came and held a meeting at which the pastor and the farmer spoke and asked the people, en masse, where they wanted to go. I thought that this was unfair and started to speak, at which point the pastor said that, in so far as I wasn't a member of their Church, I wasn't entitled to speak at their meeting. I was offended at his cheek and spoke past him saying that you can't expect a bunch of people, in two minutes, to make up their minds, collectively, where they are going.

A lady from the food-providing NGO held a training session for the leaders where she ran them through a series of 'what-if' scenarios. I was so exhausted mentally and physically that I spent most of the training session lying on my back, resting. For this I got it again, from the lady who had previously pulled me up for saying "We" when referring to SPO.

One of the babies in the community died, and the local chief gave his permission for a plot to be used in the nearby grave. Some of the young men dug a small shallow grave there. A little dolls house was placed in it and the baby buried in the doll's house. Among the mourners around the grave were three guys from the community, cracking jokes with each other. I asked my friend Kenny, what that was all about and he told me that they had been appointed to see that the proceedings didn't get too solemn

The farmer went on holiday and his foreman brought in a farmer friend who offered work to the men with partners, and two dollars and a ride to town for the single men.

That's how it finished. The couples went to the farm and worked until they found it too hard and left. The single people were dropped off at the bus station where they had been two years previously. Full circle and nothing to show for it. There was an epilogue.

A number of the former SPO guys got a small piece of land in a high density suburb outside the city, and I went to visit them. All they had was a small plot of sandy ground and I could see that they had almost no possessions. Instead of commiserating with their situation I went into an unfeeling delivery about how SPO would start again.

The youngest guy in the group got up and started to make a ritual denunciation of me. I remained quite still as he waved his arms around in close proximity to my head. When he was finished the group told me that they were finished with SPO and that they were "going with the Church", meaning the Evangelical Church, who, they said, were getting a site for them. I could see their point and got up to go; my young denunciator came with me. I took the opportunity to advise him to lower his voice a little when speaking in public and then realised that I had some money belonging to SPO at home. I went back to the group and told them this, made an arrangement to get together with them to distribute it, and departed in a friend's car.

Some days later, a former member of SPO called to our house and asked for his portion of the money. I told him that the agreement was that we were to meet, a few days hence, for it to be distributed evenly among all the people. He said that, in that case, he would put out the word that I was embezzling the money. I saw red and invited him to come to the nearby police tent, to formalise his allegation. The police officer was understanding, asked me to leave, and I let him deal with my financially anxious friend. But I was puzzled that he had been able to press my buttons so easily and effectively and concluded that I had been attached to being thought of as an honest person.

On the appointed day, one of the former leaders of SPO and I went to the high-density suburb and distributed the money. The Evangelical Church found a piece of land and some of the people moved onto it. Months later, I got a message that they wanted to see me because they were unhappy with the regime under which they were living. I went to see them and we talked. There was nothing I could do, it was someone else's show now, and I left with a sad heart. I told the lady who had driven me there that it was the emotional equivalent of divorce. And she said that that was an emotionally honest statement. Little did I know that that feeling would remain with me for two years when I got back to Ireland.

Homelessness is a product of Urbanisation, which is growing globally. Socially, mentally and physically it can be a very debilitating state. The squatters of the Street People's Organisation were a small, young group, with few skills. Unfortunately two groups were trying to organise them: one with an ecclesiastical bias and the other trying to build social democracy. There were ideological differences between these two groups and the people of SPO were in the middle, trying to survive as best they could. Ultimately the government was unprepared to allow a group of people to illegally occupy a piece of land close to downtown Harare and used heavy-handed methods to get rid of them. The people were provided with alternative land by the Evangelical Church, but didn't seem to want to become Christians. A side consequence of the burnout and ensuing events was that I didn't get my Visa and remained an illegal alien.

The Wheelbarrow
Across the open space near the Meeting House where we lived, was a restaurant. The restaurateur used to dump his waste on the open space and burn it. Consequently, there was always a light plume of smoke rising, near where people used to pass by on the path

across the open space. I took exception to this and went to the restaurateur. He laughed when I told him of my objections.

The experimental police tent was nearby and I went there, reported that my restaurateur friend was causing a public nuisance and asked them to have it stopped. Three weeks later, nothing had changed.

I went on a righteous indignation trip and got a barrow, filled it with ashes from the restaurateur's pile and dumped them right into his restaurant. I brought the kids along for the action, which was not good parenting – safety first with kids.

I left with the barrow and the kids and, having deposited them at the Meeting House, returned to the dumping scene to see how things were developing. The waiters were out in force and one of them grabbed me, thrust a shovel into my hand and commanded me to remove the ashes. I took the shovel, went into the restaurant and shovelled the ashes further in than previously. The brown stuff hit the fan and my captor grabbed me again. I could see that he was losing it and, seeing a nearby policeman, demanded to be handed into police custody

The policeman took me to the nearby police tent and the restaurateur, who spoke to the policemen with social position, soon joined us. I could see that his attitude irritated them and I felt the energy shifting in my direction. Added to this, the fact that I had reported the smoke and the police hadn't acted left them in a weak position. They released me.

Kids

The happiest times I spent in Zimbabwe, were cycling my pushbike with Cáit and Leaf on board. I discovered that children have a very high consciousness and are concerned with the big questions, like why we are here, i.e. The Meaning of Life.

Cáit put that question to me, as I was cycling her to play school one morning. Laying my Bodhisattva belief on her, I said, "You are here to save the World". In retrospect that seems a bit heavy for a four-year-old child, but when I was cycling her home that afternoon, she happily told me that she had figured out her purpose on Earth; "I'm here to save the World", she said.

Around the same time, and in a similar vein, I came home one day, to hear Leaf singing a song she had composed herself, about orbiting the Planet. It was around then that I told my girls that they were my teachers. I still hold to that opinion.

A less happy moment came on a later occasion, when they had been at school and came home in tears because they had come to realise (or had been informed) that their Parents would die some day. I was totally unprepared for this and tried to string together some insincere 'explanation'. In the end, all I could do was to share their grief with them.

There was a piano in the Meeting House and, while we were there, I wrote seven songs on it; one of them was for the kids:

Children are energy

Evolving endlessly

So, watch them and learn.

They bring serenity

Set your Spirit free

Give it back to them

Their growing bravery will often be

Integrity

Which lacks the correct quality

Of Grace

Bring them to pastures green

Back to a better scene

Back to a right place

Remember

You are dealing with spirit of the Ages

God's work

Is passing through your hands

So touch with Adoration

Your part in the Creation

Your mark in the sand

And when you are old

And passing to the grave

Look at them

And see whose Souls you've saved

They won't be just like you

But if their hearts are true

Say goodbye and wave.

The Tree

There was a tree in the garden, and from it were hanging ropes with a horizontal tyre suspended from them. The kids and I used to have fun there every night, with them sitting on the tyre and I pushing them in ever increasing circles, until they would say, "Do Magic!", at which point I would spin them too on the tyre, so that the tyre was spinning and the rope was spinning; a sort of circles within spirals scene. Then they would yell, "Do Magic!" and I would dance around, like a clown, to entertain them further.

These sessions exhausted me, though I was a young man at the time, but, you know how it is: you'll do anything for your kids, provided it is within reason and this was definitely within reason. They had a great time and I loved it, so we all got off. What more could you ask?

Smile

Cáit had a nice smile, because I was always telling her to smile. One day she came to me, with a crestfallen face and, in a plaintive voice, said to me, "Do I have to keep smiling for the rest of my Life!?" I could see her position, that was too far ahead to look for a little girl. In fact, it's too far ahead for any of us; let's live for the moment. I said no more to Cáit about smiling but she keeps it, to this day, and it is a sight to behold. A white sight that is blinding in its intensity.

Leaf has a nice smile too, but she developed it herself by imitating her sister. They are very close, yet very different in many ways. They don't fight so there is great promise in that relationship.

War and the Bishop

There was a conference at a religious centre outside Harare and a bishop spoke. During the course of his delivery he made the surprising statement that war is fun. This must be taken in the context of the fact that when the war in the country had been raging in the Rural Areas, he had been living comfortably in Harare, reading about it in the papers. Nevertheless I was furious to hear him say that and stood up and contradicted him. I lost my moxy when, later in the conference, the deputy prime minister said that when they were conducting the liberation struggle in the Rural Areas, they forcibly recruited almost every son, from every family they visited.

I thought this was slavery in the name of liberation but kept my mouth shut because I didn't want to be kicked out of the country and so joined the general conspiracy of silence in the room.

The 'Exorcism'

From time-to time since coming to the country, people had told me about the phenomenon of 'possession'. This was a state where people (usually women), were 'possessed' by spirits and danced around, in an erratic manner, waving their hands in the air and making unpleasant sounds.

I had my first experience of this one day, while walking near the intersection of First Street and Union Avenue. First Street was a pedestrian's zone and, in the middle of the intersection was a 'possessed lady', manifesting all the classic characteristics of that state.

A large circle of middle class office workers, on their lunch break and enjoying the show while they ate their rolls and drank their coffee, surrounded her. I thought this was an unhealthy situation and went up to the lady, asking her if she would like something to eat.

She answered in the affirmative and we both left the disappointed circle as its energy imploded in on itself, went to a café and had a meal. She proved to be a most congenial eating companion.

A Disobedient Government

The Commonwealth Heads of Government Meeting was due and, again, the venue was to be the Harare

Sheraton Hotel. Elizabeth Windsor, head of the Commonwealth, announced that she would like to visit a poor part of Harare and specified Mbare, a high-density suburb, which was called, 'Harare' before that name was given to the City.

Her announcement sent shivers down the collective spine of the government, because, on the route to Mbare was a squatter settlement, even bigger than that of SPO. The government told the City Council to get rid of the camp.

Maybe because they had got jam on their faces with the media when the SPO people were evicted, the government decided to go the legal route this time. The City Council applied for eviction notices on two residents of the camp, deeming that because they were leaders, everyone else would also be covered by their eviction notices. The eviction notices were granted.

I recognised that the Council was using flawed logic and checked it with a barrister friend of mine who confirmed my view. He said that if I could get a resident of the camp to take a case, he would act.

Through a friend, I succeeded in doing this and the barrister applied for an emergency hearing, which was granted.

At the hearing, which was heard by a White Judge, the two barristers stood in front of him arguing fine points of Law, in sequence, and the Judge listened carefully to the debate until he had reached a conclusion. He said that it was ironic that a government, which had come to power defending the poor, was now prepared to bury them under the red carpet. He found against Harare City Council.

However the authorities went ahead and evicted the people, in contravention of their own Courts. I don't know if Elizabeth visited Mbare, but, if she did, she would have passed a site where hundreds poor people would have been living, were it not for her desire to look at a few poor people.

Francis

Now that I was without a job, I placed an ad in one of the local newspapers, offering my engineering services. Some nights later, I was painting the bedroom with a friend, when the phone rang. It was a man called Francis Penny who was a medium sized builder. He asked me if I would go and see him in his depot the following day. He gave me directions.

The following day, we did the interview and I was asked to work on the construction of twelve small factories, six kilometres outside Harare. I had never done this work before and the foreman had, many times. Consequently, he resented this inexperienced Murungu taking over, when he had the expertise.

After a few days, when I was theoretically in charge, but the foreman was calling the shots, he was put running the job, and we became friends.

The site agent was a very competent builder but was into social position. He insisted on being called, 'Mr'. I always called him 'John', and this used to send him into paroxysms of rage, which I allowed him to manifest.

His second thing was demeaning the workers. He used to give out the pay every Friday and each delivery was invariably accompanied by a sly comment that took from the value of the work that had been performed for that money.

The clients were an Indian family and one of my jobs was to show them around each time they came to the site, which was often. They were happy with progress.

There was no first-aid box on the site and I regularly asked for one, but to no avail. The men regularly waded in concrete, because Francis didn't give them boots, which he was legally bound to do. I said this to him and he said that the only boots that would be discussed on his site would be, 'these boots are made for walking'. His meaning was clear.

I was getting fed up with this job and when Francis took my truck back because I didn't come in on a Saturday morning, having been only told about it that morning, I gave him a verbal broadside and walked off the job, getting lost on the way, because I had got so high from all the energy I had expended.

In any case, I had to go back to my Wife, tell her that another job had gone down the Swannee and, once again, see the disappointment on her face.

There was a sequel because, a few days later, I received a call from Francis' office asking me to call there. I debated whether to go or not but decided that the possibility of reconciliation over-rode other considerations. When I got there Francis and John were sitting in the office and Francis told me that he was looking for a change of attitude on my part.

I loathed what these guys stood for, so much that I just sat there with a sullen expression on my face. Recognising that he wasn't going to get the required change of attitude John told me that he would pay me my last pay packet if I went home, got my boots and brought them to him.

I went home, put the kids on the bike, and cycled back to the office and for the first time ever, I saw an expression of humanity on John's face. He saw the kids and he looked sheepish as he handed me the money.

The Job

There was to be a second sequel to the Penny Case, because, a few days after I was booted out of his camp, his client's Architect came to me and said that he had this job and he wanted me to supervise it.

There was a Friend of his up the mountains, in Chimanimani, who had a house that he wanted converted into a holiday home for rent, and he wanted me to supervise the job. He drove me there, introduced me to the owner Friend and I was left to get to know the men and start the job.

The job started and one of the guys said that he wanted
to be in charge. Every morning I rang a little bell to get
the ball rolling and though it was a little paternalistic,
the men seemed to like it because there were smiles on
their faces. Whether or not they were smiling at me, I do
not know but they seemed to like the little homilies I
gave before the job started because there was a very
good atmosphere on the job.

I started a school while I was there, in a shed at the back
of the house. The men used to come at night, after tea,
and learn how to lay bricks from the master builder we
had on site. It was a very acrimonious arrangement at
times but I used to step in, give a little demonstration on
how to behave in a classroom situation and the class
used to proceed harmoniously after that.

I let a guy who wanted to run the job run it. He put in
tremendous effort running around giving instructions.
It was telepathically obvious to all the men on site that I
was running the site but this guy was running around,
dealing with lower order concerns. Maybe I should have
made him my Deputy but I didn't because I just wanted
to run him into the ground so that I would get him out
of my hair. If I were doing it today I would handle it
differently. I would make him my deputy, give him
orders and if he couldn't handle it, I would demote him.
If he could handle it I would give him more
responsibility, within his limits.

I used to travel from Chimanimani to Harare by bus
every Friday afternoon after work, and back again every

Monday morning. One Monday morning, having alighted from the bus in the town near the job, I came across a blind busker playing the guitar and not making very much money. I took up a collection for him, gave him the money and resumed my journey. A few days later, my boss told me that he was letting me go because a businessman friend had told him that he had seen me collecting money for the busker when I should have been on the job. He obviously valued every minute of my time and social responsibility didn't come into his vision of his role in the community.

Epworth Defended
Epworth was an informal settlement outside Harare, where thousands of people lived. Its history went back as far as Cecil John Rhodes, the man who had annexed land from the Blacks, in what was to become Zimbabwe.

For his sins, he gave a piece of land to the Methodist Church and they, God Bless Them, divided it among their workers, a process which was the genesis of Epworth. Until the war of Independence, the Mission sat in the middle of these small parcels of land but then, more people fleeing the war arrived in the place and made deals with the workers, thus resulting in further subdivision.

After Independence more people, in search of the good life, headed for the city and settled in Epworth, making it a high density, informal settlement served by ground water and septic tanks.

The government wanted to improve this situation and the anecdotal evidence was that the World Bank had offered to lend the government over one hundred million dollars to upgrade the settlement.

Upgrade is a selective term because the government proposed to knock many houses, without the consent of the owners, in order to make way for roads and pipes. To oversee this operation they set up the Epworth Local Board, an organisation which, in an Irish context, would be a quango.

The plan was that the evicted people would be 'accommodated' in plastic shelters, many kilometres out the Bulawayo Road and a huge distance from their schools and jobs. It struck me as hugely ironic that a government, which had evicted the SPO from their shelters, was now building plastic shelters for people who already had houses.

I first heard about the eviction on a Saturday morning, when a friend from Epworth rang and told me that a bulldozer had started knocking houses. With a catch in my throat, I said we would sit in front of the bulldozer. In order to amplify my effort I rang 'Horizon' magazine, told them the story and asked for a photographer. Within minutes my friend, the Rasta man photographer, and a driver were around to our house and we were on the road.

The Rasta man started doing Rasta accents, as a kind of head cop strategy and I took him on with my Irish

equivalent. But he was so much better at it than I was
that I let him have the day. I said that I was going to sit
in front of the bulldozer, because of Divine
considerations.

I knew where my friend lived and we picked him up
there, from where he guided us to the demolition site.
The bulldozer was already in action. I got out of the
truck, spoke briefly to a reporter from the government
newspaper and sat in front of the bulldozer.

My faith in the humanity of the driver proved to be
justified because he stopped his motor. The foreman
asked me if I would like to speak with the district
administrator. I said I would if he would guarantee that
the bulldozer would not be switched on in my absence.
He agreed so I was driven to the DA who was standing
a discrete kilometre away from the action.

I could tell from his demeanour, that he saw himself as a
functionary doing an unpleasant job, over which he had
no control and therefore it was pointless talking to him.
I ritualistically told him to stop knocking the houses and
he said he wouldn't, so I returned to the bulldozer,
which was lying idle. I waited.

As I was waiting, leaning up against a wall, this
policeman came over to me and, in a quiet vice, said,
"Let's talk about this in private". I suspected his motive
and said that because it was a public matter, we should
discuss it in public. A cheer went up among the nearby
crowd. The bulldozer started up again and I headed

towards it. A policeman caught me by the arm and I asked him if he was arresting me but he denied it. I told him to let me go, in that case.

However, I was put into the back of a police truck which had a metal grid structure around it. The policeman in charge came around and yelled at all the gathered people to clear off. He had his back to me and, even louder, I yelled to the people to sit in front of the bulldozer and stop the eviction. This judoed him and he reeled around to see where the voice was coming from, as the truck roared off. I had asked my friend and the Rasta man to follow but they lost me.

The police van rolled into Mbare police station, within view of where Bob Marley had sung at the Independence Celebrations in 1980. Two civil servants had travelled in their own car, with the truck. The superintendent behind the counter asked them for the story and I broke in and, in a very loud voice, to get the attention of all the people in the station, told him that the government was illegally knocking down perfectly good houses and evicting people, without their consent, in Epworth. I could see all the people around me taking a keen interest in this and I could also see that the two civil servants were getting paranoid at all the attention they were getting. They backed out the door, leaving me and the superintendent to sort it out.

The superintendent put me in a cell, which was occupied by three other guys, two young and one older. The older guy started exhibiting dominant behavioural characteristics and I realised that we would have to reach an accord. I produced the cigarettes and passed them around. Instantly, he became far more amenable and we had a communal smoke.

The superintendent came around, with a smile on his face and, looking through the grill, asked me how I was feeling. He seemed to be enjoying having a captive. I said that I was feeling fine because I was following in the footsteps of Gandhi and Martin Luther King. As an afterthought, I mentioned Robert Mugabe, who, I said, had spent more time in prison than either the superintendent or I had, (I wouldn't say that today).

This seemed to do it for the superintendent. He turned away and then turned back to me telling me that he would let me go, for the week-end if I promised to return the following Monday morning. I promised and he let me go.

I took leave of my cell mates and headed in the direction of Rufaro Stadium. On the way I bought sweets and cigarettes for my cell-mates and doubled back to the police station, where I left them at the desk, because my new colleagues were nowhere to be seen. Then I went home. Soon afterwards, my Wife arrived and said that she had been touring the police stations, looking for me. I was grateful.

On the following night I received a phone call from the BBC World Service, asking for an interview and I said fine. I was in breach of the spirit of my release but I wanted to do the story on radio, to stop the eviction. The line was bad so I suggested that they take some time and then ring a friend of mine who was living in the neighbourhood. Then I rang her and asked if it would be OK. I did things in reverse order but that's the way it went down.

I had the impression that the BBCWS were looking for the negative reportage on Africa, which I loved, and went through changes in my head as to how I would handle the interview when it happened. I remained detached and offered only as little opinion as necessary, thanked my hostess and left.

On the Monday morning I returned to Mbare police station and was told that I was to be taken to another station, closer to where the eviction had happened. It took a long time for the truck to arrive, but, eventually, it came and we were off. When we arrived at the station, I was introduced to a genial assistant superintendent. He showed me into his office and left.

It was getting late and I realised that I wouldn't be able to keep an appointment I had made with a journalist, to meet him that morning. I was feeling bold and picked up the assistant superintendent's phone and rang the journalist's number. His wife told me that he was out so I gave the AS's number and asked that he ring me when he returned home.

The AS returned to the office and I told him that I had just rung a journalist. Whether he didn't believe me, or didn't care, he simply laughed and left the office again. The phone rang. It was the journalist.

I asked him did he have a tape recorder he could clip onto his phone and he said he did. We did the interview.

Eventually, the AS came back and asked me to follow him to another office. In that office I met a detective inspector, who was in civvies

I told him that the Ministry of Home Affairs was using its police officers as bailiffs when they should be police officers and he agreed with me. I said he should be talking to the Minister for Home Affairs about it and he said that this was not possible but asked me to do it. I said that I would. He released me.

In the following few days, I rang the Ministry for Home Affairs twice, but there was no answer so my barrister friend and I initiated a Court case.

Our position was, that there was no legal basis for the Epworth Local Board and that therefore the evictions were illegal. We won the case and the evictions stopped.

'Homeless News'

Arising out of my commitment to homeless people, I decided to start a newsletter, which would give the stories of people begging on the streets of Harare. I asked a former SPO friend of mine and he gave it his blessing. I decided to call the newsletter, 'Homeless News' and the publishers 'Oh, to Have a Little House'

Publications, from the first line of Pádraic Colum's poem, 'An Old Woman of the Roads'.

On reflection, the decision to start this venture was a bit colonial, in so far as I was a visitor to the country and didn't have the right to start checking for dust on the mantelpiece. That was their job.

The same could be said of my other work for people threatened with eviction but then, when you see a wrong about to be committed, what are you to do? Are you an Irish citizen or a Planetary one? I prefer Planetary.

For the first edition, my routine was straightforward. I went around the streets of the City and wrote down the stories of people I met, some of them blind and sitting on the pavement. A guy in a local NGO agreed to format the stories and another NGO ran them off.

In the second edition I wrote the story of the bulldozing at Epworth, and how the police didn't want to perform the role of bailiff. This was before the Court case. I brought one hundred copies of the newsletter to Parliament and left a named copy for each member of the House of Representatives.

My Wife and I had recently divorced and, with my agreement, she had just brought the girls back to Ireland. Plane tickets were getting expensive and a quick move was necessary. I knew that my Parliamentary move would probably increase the heat in my life and I think it represented a kind of final statement, when I knew that I wouldn't be around much longer. I didn't expect a free ticket home but that is what I got.

Deportation

A few days after my Parliamentary visit, I got home (some friends had moved into the Meeting House and were putting me up), to be told that two men had called looking for me and had left a telephone number. I called the number, spoke to one of the men and was asked to call to the Immigration Office the following day, which I did.

When I got there I was told that I was being detained, pending deportation to Ireland. I was asked to call a friend, who would get my stuff together and bring it to the office. I rang her.

With my detaining officer, we went to the bank and I withdrew my money. On the way back, my friend held my hand.

I had made out a list of all the things I wanted, including a 150mm length of dope, which I had hidden at home, but my friend said I shouldn't have included it on the list as it might be seen. She rubbed it out.

I was brought to a Remand Prison outside Harare and given prison garb to wear. The Prison consisted of a large yard, surrounded by an array of large cells, each with a capacity for forty prisoners. Dotted around the yard were uniformed prison officers.

A practice that surprised me was one where a prisoner would approach a guard and shine his shoes, while the officer looked down, impassively. It seemed that this ritual had spilled over from the UDI days and that now it was Black on Black.

Each cell had a head prisoner and his job was to ensure that all his inmates were accounted for at the end of each day. This involved lining everyone up in a squatting position each night, and counting heads. I refused to join initially, because our head prisoner was coming on like Hitler. But when he ameliorated it I relented and subjected myself to the head count. After that, there was no friction between us.

Visits were allowed, through the perimeter wire fence, which reminded me of the Basketball scene, from *West Side Story*. Some members of my Men's Group paid a visit and I entertained them with a song from the show; just to let them know that I was OK.

They gave me food and I was blessed because it was better than the prison food, which was cooked in vats, over a metre high.

There was a room set aside for prisoners who had been given food by visitors. The drill was that these prisoners would share their food so that one finished up eating more of the other people's food than one's own.

On day three of my prison stay, I was given back my own clothes and was taken by car to Harare International Airport. The plane was delayed so I was taken to a nearby Police Station, to be detained overnight.

There was a boy in the cell with me and I had him doing press-ups, to keep fit. I don't know what my propensity for getting kids to do press-ups is, but I suppose it is about getting them to be fitter than I was, though I was pretty fit at their age.

The Sergeant arrived and seemed pleased that his prisoner had found a mentor. I was pleased that he was pleased because he could have seen it as an act of oppression. His wisdom was apparent. I was taken to the Airport.

At the Airport, I met the media. I had hipped my friends to get them there for the departure and, sure enough, they turned up.

There was a bit of trickery there, because I had told the guy who was looking after me at the Airport that my friends were going to turn up and could I see them.

He let me go out into the Departures Lounge, and there I met my friends and a few people from the media.

I gave an interview, talked to my friends, and then my minder came out to see that the rooster had flown the nest and that the information was out there, in the media. The plane arrived and I was taken on board, without my passport, which was given to the captain. I asked for it back, on the basis that it was the property of

the Irish Government and it was handed back to me
with bad grace.

When the plane landed in Gatwick, I was interviewed
by two people from Security and they laughed when I
told them the story. I took a plane to Dublin and a train
to Cork. When I landed in Cork I was met by Sean, Adi
and Owen.

If I was a bit hard on the Authorities I regret it, and if I
was hard on my friends I regret that also. I loved
Zimbabwe and I loved the people there.

Part 2:

Stigma and Mental Health

Presentation at the Gilbert Centre, Mallow

By

Declan Gould

Monday February 7th 2011

Good evening friends

The Mental Health Movement of Ireland is growing with both Yin and Yang qualities in it. Isn't it the same with all of us? What is stigma? According to Collin's Dictionary, it is a distinguishing mark of social disgrace. I suggest it is also an attitude of disapproval or hostility: looking down our noses at someone or group. That sort of thing. In this regard I feel we all have a bit of visual adjustment to do.

Who are the victims? Jews during Nazi Germany; those with the 'wrong' address; wrong accent; 'wrong' job or no job; city people living in the country and vice versa; old people; young people; people who don't look too good; rich people; poor people; politicians; travellers; gypsies. Is there anyone left? Celebrities? Are they the de facto Icons of our society!
Stigma is a state of mind and therefore it can be changed.

Stigmatic Mini Buses

One thing I see from time to time is a mini bus, with the name of some philanthropic business people's organisation on it, ferrying kids around; the clear subtext being, "These kids are different and aren't we good for helping them?"

"Let them have their publicity" some may argue. "Not at the expense of the kids" I would answer.

Struggling Souls

There are struggling souls in the Psychiatric Institutions of this country and it is for these people that a growing number is speaking out. These souls are largely ignored by our society and excluded from the maelstrom by virtue of their secluded lifestyle and economic circumstances. Integrative work needed, but ask a nurse if she would like to come for a coffee and usually the professional guillotine will come crashing down.

The Stigmatic Dance

In Hindu philosophy Life is likened to a Dance; the Lila. This corresponds to science's concept of matter as vibrating energy. Modern social dancing is freer than its predecessors; anyone may dance with anyone else and anyone, male or female, may initiate a dance. In this sense the Health service is back in the days of the céilí: staff over here; clients over here; advance retire; advance retire; keep the mixing to a minimum. It's a bipolar social system which teaches you to know your place determined by whether you arrived in your own car or in a squad car.

By the way, I'm not down on céilí, per se. I used to do it in my courting days and loved it.

The Stigmatic World

How do we deal with stigma, that amorphous mind set which can be as much in the head of the sufferer as in that of the general public? Turn it upside down. Make it cool to have been in hospital. That's what Mad Pride is all about. This is not a new thing. The Quakers were given the term 'Quaker' as a derogation of the fact that they 'quaked' when speaking the truth. They simply accepted the term and, four hundred years later, still use it.

Another example is when some of the Hippies, in San Francisco in the Sixties, started calling the Police 'pigs'. The Police responded by wearing smiling porky pig epaulettes on their sleeves and going around being nice to people. Upturn the stigma and be proud of it. After all it was hard earned. Make Change; See Change. Makes sense.

Bus Stops
Regularly I talk to people at bus stops and, if the conversation is flowing in the right direction I tell them of my conversion from madness to sanity. They immediately reassure me that I don't seem mad to them, which reassures me that I was on the right track. From time to time one of them tells me that they have a relative who was in hospital or that they themselves have been. If we are to build a community of the formerly and presently wounded, and others, wherever we meet them, we must be prepared to link up with people; receive their blessings and return them with ours.

Low spirits
We are all familiar with the cough mixture ad which shows this guy walking around with a cloud over his head; low spirits; low self esteem; suffering from a cold condition, which is then cured by a tincture of a

proprietary product. It may work on television but blowing away stigmatic feelings is not so simple if one is in low spirits.

I know a guy who wouldn't go to the Mad Pride event in Fitzgerald's Park in Cork in case he was seen.

Employment

Similarly, applying for a job is tricky if one is inclined to stick to the literal truth. How does one account for the time spent in hospital and recuperation? Bend the truth. Tell them one was looking after the family. It's no business of a potential employer what goes on in one's personal life.

Small Initiatives

There are people who are so medicated and institutionalised that their powers of speech are virtually gone. They are actually limitless. But they have virtually no voice. This is why we in Glenmalure, an HSE house where I live, in Cork, started 'Glenmalure and Friends' magazine, aimed at people who are in receipt of mental health services. It is a high quality magazine and, to date, has had great success in reaching its target audience.

Similarly, a number of Friends and I have started 'The Next Step', an organisation to offer arts and crafts skills to those who have been in hospital. It is also our intention to find premises where our participants can sell their work, thus augmenting their income. At present we have located training premises and a teacher, and are recruiting the first ten people to participate in a ten week trial run. We in 'Glenmalure and Friends' and 'The Next Step' encourage others to start small projects which will ease the burden, or make life more meaningful for those who are swimming upstream at present.

Language and Stigma

People in power are infamous for misusing the language for their own ends. The American military and the CIA invented the terms 'collateral damage' and 'extraordinary rendition' to disguise, from the conscious minds of people, the fact that they were talking about killing and transportation for torture, respectively. This indicates, at least, that they were aware of public sensibilities. However, that didn't change the practice; merely the terminology.

What's also distasteful is the way our broadcasters, who are paid by our taxes, slavishly follow the CIA line as if they were talking about inadvertently breaking cups or the performance of a musical piece, when they are actually talking about human suffering and death. I am sure you will join me in giving a collective thumbs down to that practice.

Medical Codes

Medics also have their codes. The first one I encountered was the term 'flat'. It sounds inconsequential and I suggest that's why it is used so regularly. 'Flat', as used by medics, in my experience, can mean anything from 'bland' to 'languishing in the

depths of hell'. I was in the latter state one time, due to
an inappropriately heavy regime of medication. I told
my medic about it and she casually said, "We won't
keep you flat for very much longer". It was a double
whammy. It was bad enough to be in the condition I
was in without it being implicitly denied in such a blasé
way. Furthermore, where was this "for very much
longer" coming from? Why was I there in the first place?

Another word which, medically used, gives me cause
for concern; it is the word, 'present', as in, "He
presented to the doctor with a head ache". He presented
what? Himself? Then why not say it? Because people
don't present themselves to each other under normal
circumstances. They meet. But this is not a normal
circumstance. It's a visit to the doctor so it gets special
language, even though it breaks the rules of normal
usage. It's not just that, but the term has regal overtones
which, I say, have no place in the medical surgery. You
may think it's a small point, however, I present it to you
for your consideration.

The Irish Scene
I can't speak about Irish psychiatry at large, because,
probably like many here, I have had only a limited
experience of it. From the points of view of Design,
Maintenance and Quality of Care, it has been a disaster
at times and great at times; love being the mitigating
factor. I hear stories of serious neglect, in run-down
buildings. For me, It could have been a lot worse and it

could have been a lot better, but if these stories are real we'd better do something about it, fast.

Cork

I live in Cork City and there the building most in need of extensive upgrading is St Catherine's, in St Finbarr's Hospital, on the Douglas Road. It's not quite as much a home as an institution. Glenmalure has a lot of positive features. Not because I am in Mallow am I saying this but, in my limited travels, the most attractive community dwelling I have come across is Solas Nua, here in this town. But it isn't just the architecture that's relevant; it's also the relationship between staff and residents. Bonding counts and I have done lots of it, as well as the reverse.

Impeccability or Stigma

Staff are paid to be impeccable in their behaviour but they needn't be because they are staff. Clients aren't but they had better be because they are regularly judged by a corps of people whose concepts of normality, as one would expect, vary from individual to individual and who, for the consultant, can record their subjective observations as if they were inscribing holy writ. Practically speaking, it is holy writ because it can determine whether or not one passes through the portal to Nirvana.

The Mental Health Movement and Pharmacopeia

Speaking of the Mental Health Movement in our country. From where I am looking, it is coalescing, though it is early days. The organisational style we have

at present is the one we want; decentralised, issue
orientated; otherwise we wouldn't have it. I don't want
a monotone organisation with layers of beaurocracy
where the member gets lost.

We are building a movement which is a precious thing
and requires great care in getting it and keeping
together. Our goal is mental health which has in it
elements of free thought and free expression. We ought
to espouse influences which would gag this free flow.
Pharmacopoeia is an old Art but we shouldn't be
overcome by it.

Sanity is our goal and our aim.

Declan P Gould

Part 3 : Under Observation -
A Patient View from the Psychiatric Ward

by

Declan Gould

Note on abbreviations used:

PC = patient community

PE = psychiatric establishment

GF = psychiatric ward in Cork University Hospital (CUH)

Authenticity: The way it's set up at present, this guy has the right, alone, to tell you whether you are authentic or not and the whole of society buys into 'his' reality. Too much power. However, *the times they are a changing?*

Authority, Legitimate/Rational: For authority to be legitimate it must have the consent and confidence of those who have delegated responsibility to it. Patients should not be forced to go to a doctor they dislike or distrust; it's non-therapeutic.

Back to Education: A fine idea; bringing PC people into a benign learning environment. However, for some, the level of education provided is well below their standards of attainment. Also, *most of the graduates graduate to unemployment.*

Beating oneself up: This can happen when one realises that one is trapped and feels that it one's own fault, though one can't exactly trace the cause-effect chain which led to one's present situation.

Be nice: You have been taken in, against your will; likewise medicated; and you are expected to be nice. *How real is that?*

Biology-led therapy: Based on the belief that we are merely biological organisms. While tablets can affect consciousness so do Prayer, Meditation and good actions. Is consciousness biological? Maybe, but it takes more than tablets to keep it together.

Bi-lateral conversations in a tri-angular situation: Quite frequently, docs and nurses discuss the future of the patient in 'his/her' presence, without any involvement of the Patient. *This is unprofessional and should be addressed.*

Bipolar, popularity of: In a recent and novel development, it is becoming quite fashionable to be 'bi-polar' (witness Sinead O'Connor and Catherine Zeta Jones e.g.). This is indicative of the early stages of the breakdown of stigma and is to be welcomed. If you've got it you may as well flaunt it.

Blood Pressure: At regular intervals you will have your blood pressure taken to determine whether it is high or low. These are indicators of many possible conditions

Blood Samples, forced: The PE can force you to give a blood sample, in search of the presence of illicit drugs in your bloodstream.

Blood Tests: Taken to ascertain the presence of various drugs; elements and other substances in the bloodstream. These tests can evoke a reading which tells if the substances are present within the 'therapeutic range'

Blues, the, and Global Warming: Is anyone looking at the possible connection between our chronic environmental situation, despair and rising suicide rates among the young. Seems obvious. Is there anything about it out there from the Tasks Forces?

Boredom: In hospital, large swathes of the day are featureless, with Patients forced to either sit smoking in the smoking shelter, or sit in the day-room watching television, talking, or in silence. Rest can be good, but how much can you take? In GF, Relaxation 'Exercises' and Art Therapy are available but that's only 2 hours out of a sixteen-hour day. How much of the Budget goes into Salaries?

Branded Unemployable: For some, especially long-stay Patients, it can be difficult to get back into the workforce when one leaves hospital, for psychological as well as other reasons (tablets). There are Job Coaches to help one navigate this journey.

Budget, Political. The relative importance of Mainstream and Mental Health-Care can be gauged by their respective per-capita Budgets. Mainstream Healthcare Patients are represented by the Irish Patients Association which has a high profile. The high-profile Organisations working on behalf of the PC are the Irish Advocacy Network; SHINE and Mental Health Reform.

Bullying: Bullying happens in hospital. If you have been bullied, contact your Advocate and take it from there.

Business Company: A system of administration where all the major decisions are made by one, almost never seen, person. For the patient, life on the ward can be akin to this; living under total control, including what chemicals are put into one's system and how one feels. The carrot is the hope that one will feel well in time and that the company will change.

Capitalism; money before people: Money talks; is that why some PC people don't talk much?

Carpentry: In GF, CUH, for years, there was a fully equipped Carpentry Work-Shop at the disposal of the Patients, under the supervision of a qualified Carpenter. It was shut down, "due to Insurance and Health-and-Safety reasons". It could have been replaced with a more benign activity space; e.g. wood carving.

Chakras: People don't like elated people, that is why we finish up in hospital and have our chakras chemically shut down.

Change: Properly implemented change takes time, so we are in this for the long haul. Let's keep an eye on who benefits from the change.

Checks and Balances: Diminishing in these times of austerity, but still present.

Church: In some ways the PE is a Church, with cardinals, bishops, priests, brothers and sisters. It has its own orthodoxies and is anointed by the State, *which makes it an Established Church.*

Cigarettes: The Hospital Economy: the de- facto secondary currency in hospital, is tobacco. It is talked about; bartered; compared; and of course smoked in the smoking shed, by strangers who are out of their minds for something to do and talk about.

Clinical: This is the word which confers an aura of objectivity on a PE person's opinion; ("He is clinically insane" e.g). It means little other than that a trained person deems it to be so.

Clothes washing machine-GF: There is no clothes washing machine in GF-CUH. Patients are expected to take their washing, wrapped in bed-sheets, across the road to the mile-away Laundry. A coin-operated machine on the ward would easily do the trick.

Co-dependency: "I can't do without you and you can't do without me"; a sticky path. The PE depends on the PC to maintain its lifestyle and the PC depends on the PE to maintain its headspace in reasonable order. It would be nice if the lifestyles were more alike.

Coffee & Coke: Patients consume prodigious quantities of caffeine, in dilute form. Could this be to give them a lift when medicated to a downward state? Could it be to flush the tablets out of their systems? Could it be both? It is conjecture but the answer may be in the affirmative.

Collective Delusion: There, is an assumption among some that capitalism is the best way to run the world. There is a growing belief amongst others that it may be the worst way to ruin the world. We are supposed to be a Human Family; no-one would run a Family where most of the goodies float to the top.

Community: Generally we are gregarious, and sharing the human spirit with each other can be healing. Some have the periodic contrary need for solitude. For those forcefully within, the only place for solitude is 'the bed', if they let you go there.

Competence: To avoid becoming a total 'drone', it is necessary to have some saleable skill; if the PE encourages people to come to 'therapy classes' why not give them something to make which will fetch a price?

Complementary Health Therapies: Well-off people are queuing up for them, at hotels, resort and spas. These people are not fools; they know what they are getting and are prepared to pay for it. Not available on the medical card, however.

Concentration: Many members of the PC are unable to concentrate for long, due to tablets. This makes it difficult for them to hold down a job in the mainstream. Therefore, sheltered employment, e.g. making craft objects, is suggested. This would provide a small extra income, the company of one's peers and the dignity that earning confers.

Conflict, the Legitimacy of: Non-violent behaviour does not necessarily exclude conflict of idea or interests. The PE-PC continuum includes such tension, primarily in relation to the right to incarcerate vs. the desire to get out. At present this can only be resolved by approved behaviour or by reference to the Mental Health Tribunal

Confusion: Many people arrive (under duress), at the local 'Acute Unit' with a pretty clear belief in their state of consciousness. In most cases, having seen the PE member, they are landed with a stigma, which, coming from an 'authority', leads to astonishment, confusion and loss of self-belief. It doesn't have to be like that: self-belief is more important than the opinion of another person, unless that person is a friend and your PE person probably won't be your friend. Counseling is better than labeling.

Consciousness and tablets: Tablets work: they can bring you up or down, depending on the type and dose. They can also give you consequences you don't want i.e. dull your thinking; make you drool; give you the shakes. Unfortunately, the only person who can try to do something about this is the person who gave them to you in the first place, so, if dissatisfied, immediately repair to the PE person who gave you them.

Consultations: 5-15 minutes: There is a queue waiting outside; this is your quota; prepare for it in advance. It is good to make notes in advance, so as to get to the point as soon as possible and to stick with it. You deserve no less.

Counteractive drugs: There are drugs which combat the unwanted effects of other drugs. Do they also have unwanted effects?

Cultural authenticity: A stigma can be a heavy load, unless one seeks out the company of one's fellows in the PC and in other places where one is accepted.

Culture and income: Ivan Illich coined the phrase 'Knowledge Stock', whereby some people are transmuting their information and energy into cash whereas others are converting theirs into service of the community.

Criticism as Therapy: Most of us have been on the receiving end of it. Talk back; you too have your story and it needs to be heard.

Crushed resolve: It is possible, given the unassailable authority-structure one finds oneself in within the walls of hospitals, for ones spirit to go down the tubes. Take time to yourself; call your Advocate; Talk to your Key Worker; talk to an understanding friend.

Declining Tablets: You are entitled to decline tablets, if you feel they are adversely affecting you. However you would be advised to discuss this with your PE person as soon as possible.

De-energisation and de-humanisation: Personal energy is an imperative. Some have more that they need and others have less than they want. Energy wise, the PE often puts members of the PC in a down place and leaves them there until they are allowed up in a controlled chemical way. This puts the PC in a weird place and even their own friends leave them alone

Dependence, Independence, Interdependence: The current wisdom within the PE is to 'move people towards Independent living'. Let's hope that this isn't a one-solution fits-all philosophy as there are those right along the Dependence, Independence, Interdependence spectrum out there all the time.

Desk, The: As every bureaucrat knows, sitting behind a desk can create an aura of objectivity and legitimacy, particularly for the person sitting at the other side of the desk.

Dialogue: The PE is highly trained to act as a unit, which is why it is so hard to move; only countervailing united PC can engage to make the necessary differences.

Dignity, Respect for: Would any member of the PE put a member of their family into a public psych acute unit?

Director of Psychiatric Services HSE: There is a new Director of Psychiatric Services in the HSE. The buck stops there

Does he take sugar?: The Title of a BBC Radio 4 Programme, in the past. Well meaning people can commit faux pas and talk about you in your presence as if you weren't there. Register you presence.

Drooling: This is a consequence of a particular drug.

Drugs and Fertility (Female): There are drugs which interfere with a woman's ability to have babies.

Drugs, detoxing: it is the common aspiration of the PC to quit its drugs; (some champions have done so). Only to be done with cooperation of one's PE person.

Duty of Care and Hanging out with PC: In hospital, you will quickly find out that the PE aren't your friends; they hang out together most of the time, and spend little time with the PC. You are better off, unless otherwise necessary, not seeking their attention. If you approach them looking for a little attention, they will: lapse into silence and freeze you out; or carry on talking to each other, ignoring you. Let them be.

ECT: Electro convulsive therapy: Based on the observation that people with epilepsy don't suffer from depression, and on the conclusion that if a depressed person is given a simulated epileptic seizure their depression will go away; a peculiar form of logic but some medics claim it works. There is an International controversy raging about this at present.

Elation and Giftedness: Elated people can be very gifted with acute perception and speed of thought but they don't know when to sit back and give the other person a chance.

Emotional Distress: Can be innate or caused by the drugs the consultant is experimenting with to re-establish 'balance'.

Emotional Trauma and Marriage: The tricky business of integrating emotional trauma with relationship / marriage causes many of them to fall apart. It has been reported that only 8% of 'bi-polar marriages' succeed; mainly due to the diligence of the un-affected party.

Employability again: It isn't necessarily the case that you won't get your old job back when you come out of hospital, especially if you work for a public body and have a contract

Energy: You may find your energy levels drop, due to the drugs you are on. This can lead to a drop in thinking speed and speed of action. You may find difficulty to do previously easy tasks. There are two courses of action open to you: see your PE person or accommodate yourself to the new reality by dropping unnecessary actions and focusing on your core tasks.

Energy Levels, Relative: It isn't difficult for the PE staff to maintain control in the ward, because they have more energy than the PC. This is mainly due to the drugs regime operating there.

Entropy and Listlessness: According to some scientists, the Universe is on its way to total energy 'flatness', (entropy), where it will be all the same where ever you go. This is the reality many patients experience in hospital, either innately or through drugs. Pharma should know better.

Equality of opportunity: there is a Law which says that 3% of government employees can be 'disabled'. This Law isn't policed and therefore isn't implemented

Evidence: Your psychiatrist can declare you 'unfit to give evidence' in a Court of Law, even where 'he' is the Plaintive.

Expertise and the PC: There are many gifted people in the PC. For increased political clout, the Art of running some meetings needs to be improved.

Eyes Cast Ahead Psychiatry: The PE coasts along the hospital corridors, apparently oblivious to the fact that there are patients around, who would like to share eye contact, at least. A medical acquaintance of mine says that if they don't keep their attention fixed, on the wall ahead, they will never get there. What's more important; the wall or the patient?

Eyes Cast Down Psychiatry: This is where you enter the psychiatrist's office and are assessed in an instant. The remainder of the transaction consists of you answering questions while the psychiatrist records her impressions of where you are at, eyes cast down, in 'the notes'.

Families: Families can get tied up in knots at the communication level. This can lead to one member (maybe the most perceptive) being 'put inside'. Maybe the family needs to sort itself out, collectively, by agreement of course, but this doesn't happen often. We need to get on with our families

Family Rooms: The present visitor arrangement in GF isn't adequate for family visits; crowded; too up in each other's faces; no privacy.

Fear and the PE: When faced with a member of the PE, someone who has the capacity to change one's consciousness, one can experience fear; especially if one is already satisfied with one's state of mind. This is quite convenient to the PE because then you are easier to handle.

Fees and private treatment: This can be €100 per hour at the lower end of the scale

Fellowship and the PC: At one level the fellowship within the PC is a boon: mutual support; collective of like-minded spirits. At another, mainly for economic and societal reasons, it can be an inward-looking set. This is where Social Protection and Work in Therapy Centres should be entering the picture. It's either more therapy or more work.

Females, the ascent of: As in other professions: Law, Teaching e.g. the PE is being increasingly occupied by females. Does this mean we can expect an increased level of compassion (the 'feminine dividend')? Time will tell.

Feng Shui and Hospitals: Feng Shui is the Art of marrying physical surroundings to the emotional, spiritual and practical needs of occupants.

Free Travel: A boon to the PC, which, generally, doesn't own cars and therefore has a lower carbon footprint.

Freedom: It is noteworthy that for a value called freedom, there are those whose exercise of that commodity is limited by compounds which are administered in the name of health.

Friends and Stigma: if one continues to be weird after hospital, friends can disappear.

Friends in the PC Sub-culture: Many people who go into hospital find that when they come out a large percentage of their friends (all, in some cases) are from the PC. It's a loose Network but is tighter in organisations like The Basement Resource Centre; AWARE; GROW; the Consumer Panels of the NSUE

Friendly PEs: It is possible to be friendly and be a psych. And there such people around, but that doesn't change the system which is iniquitous.

Frustration: this can be a side effect of life on the ward, with nothing to do.

Glasnost and Perestroika: You won't have any input into your notes and if you want to see them you won't be allowed, under Law. Anyway, who wants to read someone else's subjective views of you?

Graceful behaviour: This is an (unspoken) goal, on the Ward. It's harder to achieve it when one has drugs coursing through one's veins and brain.

Greed: Is greed insane?

Greed is good: A line from Michael Douglas, in the movie, 'Wall Street'.

Group Support: Patients provide each other with a lot of support. At times they become source of frustration to each other, so close is the space they occupy.

Guards, The: Authorised by Law to bring someone to a hospital. Only a consultant can incarcerate a person in hospital.

Habits, Personal Routine: The necessity of constantly having to invent one's life. Courses are OK; therapy is OK; but suitable work is best. Money in the pocket and a decent quality of life

Habits: Repetitive actions which either make us feel well or otherwise.

Happiness/Elation: These are on a continuum topping out at ecstasy (not the tablets). Ecstasy is a very dangerous state and can lead to personal and social disintegration; also to a very unpleasant drug regime.

Health and Safety: Necessary, though often over-applied, Codes of Practice

Heaven-and-Hell: The sequential worlds inhabited by those with 'bi-polar`. Medication can be effective but good habits and suitable work is also helpful. Meaning in one's life and a good quality of life can help modulate the condition.

Heisenberg Effect: Patients (and nurses), in wards are aware that they are under observation and their resultant self consciousness can alter their behaviour. Consequently, when the 'notes' arrive on the psychiatrist's desk, they describe the behaviour of someone whose conduct was conditioned by the medical model.

Holidays: When the PE is on holiday, it's not; it's 'away'.

Housework: Don't frazzle yourself doing it. If you are deep in the blues, get a carer.

Human Rights and Communication: In lock-up facilities your mobile phone will be taken away though you will still have (optional) access to a land-line. Is this unconstitutional?

Hunger, Weight Gain and Tablets: Many drugs cause an increase in appetite and in weight. This can make people unattractive and this can be seen as evidence of malpractice by the PE.

Identity and Stigma: Stigma is a demeaning attitude towards a member of the PC, either from within or from others. Development of one's talents, mutual support, are routes to follow. They can lead to confidence.

Identity, Loss of and Drugs: Drugs can lead to a radical alteration in one's mind set. It's hard to adapt to a new head space and it requires a lot of support.

Impeccability: There are people out there getting away with behaviour which the PC would not be allowed. When you have the stigma you've got to be careful.

Incarceration, Forceful: Let's call a spade a spade; you can't 'admit' a person into a space against their will, (as in 'involuntary admission'). Admission requires both parties to be willing.

Independent Living: The direction in which the PE is moving the PC; not suitable for all. Some prefer community living. It's a cash-modulated process.

Indignation: An initial reaction towards being given a stigma. Having a stigma and being on sedatives can be like grieving for one's lost self.

Inertia and Drugs: Some drugs make it very hard to get up and go and consequently, to interact with one's fellows or perform conventional work. The healing Arts have a huge job to do.

Information Flow: The PE generally asks questions and the PC answers them, so they know far more about you than you do about them (they even write notes about your thoughts). The very rare nurse comes along who lets you into her life and she is appreciated.

Inquisition: Rapid-fire questions from some of the PE.

Insanity as Sin: It is possible, while elated, to commit social faux pas, which, in retrospect, lead to guilt and a sense of having sinned. This is the depression phase of the cycle but, in turn, disappears for a while.

Intelligence and Tablets: Many tablets reduce thought-rate, and consequently, intelligence

Intimidation: The carrot-and-stick are part of ward-governance, generally. It's about yin and yang in the service of order, which can cause to lots of disorder in the minds of the PC.

It's OK to not feel OK: Mantra used by some counsellors.

Job coach: This is someone who checks you out to see if 'he' can find a job for you which suits your requirements.

Keeping it together: The PE hasn't got the answer to all your unpleasant inner states. One such case is if you are depressed but are 'bi-polar'. The PE will not give you an anti-depressant lest you get elated, so you just have to live with the depression, until it lifts.

Key Worker System: Each patient is assigned a nurse-counselor on a daily basis, who is available to them for short-duration counseling sessions, as the need arises.

Language: Every profession has its characteristic language and vocabulary. However, it is or should be incumbent upon it to communicate with its clients in an intelligible manner.

Lethargy: A lethargic life isn't as full of vitality as a lived life. We have got to change the system to let in alternative treatments, if only on a trial basis.

Line managers: A term imported from the industrial world, (as in 'production line'). Where is the line and what's on it? The line is the ward and you are on it. You are being 're-cycled', chemically born again.

Lock-up Facility: This is for sinners who don't show sufficient grace on the 'Acute Ward'. The 'Facility' is locked in inclement weather and there is nothing to do except lie on one's bed. When the sun comes out, the outside lock is unlocked and inmates pour into the 'garden' (a small patch of grass surrounded by a 12 ft high fence). When the rains come, the patients are locked up again.

Love: Patients fall in love, but it is difficult as there is no privacy.

Lovely Weather, isn't it? This is the five-second greeting of the in-coming nurse, at the start of the shift, before 'he' disappears to join his fellows in the nurses' office.

Mad/bad? Is Mad bad? It's certainly inconvenient for all concerned but does it justify incarceration, medication and loss of confidence? We need better therapies. The allopathic method, while partly successful, needs to be expanded into a more holistic therapeutic approach or supplanted completely.

Madness and community: If unity is the opposite of madness, there are many strands of madness coursing through our society, because clearly, it does not behave in a completely united fashion. Who draws the line? The Judiciary does and the PE. Who anoints the Judiciary? The political classes do. Who appoints the PE? It does, itself; it's a self-reproducing organism.

Madness and public Confession: There is a philosophy abroad that 'telling your story' in public is beneficial. It may be beneficial for the audience but for some of the story tellers, it is a very painful experience.

Madness; a religion of one: A term coined a long time ago. The 'mad' person has 'his' own perceptions; beliefs and speech patterns and can neither relate nor be related to. In Ireland these people used be called, 'Daoine le Dia', 'People of God'. Today's PE philosophy is less reverent.

Management: Who are they? : It's quite common, on the ward, for unpopular rules to be ascribed to 'management', without ever specifying who management is. This is unnecessary. Management is the clinical director in charge of the ward.

Manhandling with impunity: A nurse is empowered to manhandle you with impunity. It's called restraint and there is a debate going on about it at present.

Medical Library UCC: If you qualify for readership at UCC Library, your application for access to the medical library will go before the board.

Medievalism: The PE-PC continuum is structured like Medieval society: Lords and Ladies (with radical powers to incarcerate); Soothsayers (who know the potions); Vassals (who dispense these potions) and Serfs who carry the load of the lot, in their heads. We must evolve out of this. A more collegiate approach would do for a start.

Meditation, Guided: A mind relaxation method where participants lay on mats on the floor and follow the music and the voice of the person guiding the meditation.

Mental Health and Justice: it has been said that the word of a psychiatrist is enough to prevent a person from participating in a court case as a witness. If true, it means that such a person is being deprived of their judicial rights.

Mental Health and Social Justice: Arguably, most members of the PC are not in employment and are receiving 'Disability Allowance' of €203. This allows for basic survival but insures a very paltry quality of life.

Mind and matter: it is undoubtedly true that certain chemicals can affect the mind, which must mean that mind and matter are on a continuum.

Mind Control and the PE: The PE is about mind and behaviour control, either through chemically induced thought modification or through the implication that if one doesn't 'straighten up' one will be inside again.

Missing Link, The: ' A Vision for Change' envisages multi skill teams, sitting all over the country handing out 'Care Plans' for people who come into their radar. There is no plan for Work to be part of the Care Plans. This is the 'missing link'

Money, more: Even Donald Trump wants more money. The PC could be a force in the economy, if it were introduced to appropriate work. Any brainpower in the PE willing to work this one out?

Mysticism: Implicitly, mysticism claims that meditation is the road to non-suffering and enlightenment. Try telling that to someone with the deep blues.

Negotiation (with consultant): Impossible if one doesn't know the facts. The facts you know are how you are feeling. Let them be known, clearly.

New Crop: There are new nurses coming off the University production line now. There is some evidence to suggest that they will be more interactive with the PC, though it could be early days prior to life in the office filling forms and writing notes.

Next Step: A liberal PC-conceived Arts-and-Crafts experience.

Night Lights: A very unsettling practice whereby the night-nurse comes around, early in the morning and shines a torch in your eyes to see if you are alive. It can take hours to get back to sleep after this one.

Non-communicators: generally, the nursing staff keeps itself to itself, in the nurses' office. Even if one approaches them to 'chew the fat' one will be stone-walled, given the cold shoulder, as seems to be part of nurses' training to have as little as possible to do with patients. Reciprocate in kind.

Non-violence: Some messages will be delivered in a loud voice, in your direction, from the PE. If appropriate, reciprocate with as much skill as you can muster under the circumstances. Your self-respect is at stake

Normality: For some, normality is about sitting in an office, asking people what's going on in their heads; for others it's about answering those questions. There is no universal norm except breathing, speaking, eating and another small number of things we share.

Notes, The: While on the ward, you will be scrutinised (usually from a distance) by the nurses and your 'performance' will be evaluated and noted, on a daily basis, in a folder, known colloquially as 'the notes'. Some nurses have said that their main motivation, while writing "the notes", is "to cover their own asses" i.e. to describe any incident in a way that reflects well on them.

Nurse-Doctor Dynamics: Bi-lateral conversations in a triangular situation; the doctor tells the nurse that 'she' is going to "send him on a course", with no reference to you, or to your preferences for your life. Some of them are actually like that.

Obesity: Exercise and trying to stem the tide of fat bulging out of one's body, which can be a consequence of taking tablets. Pharma hasn't solved this one yet.

Objectivity: Objectivity depends on ones point of view; however the more agreement one has with the greatest number of people, the greater the chance of an objective opinion existing.

Observers: The time the nurses get closest to the patients is at mealtimes when they stand, at the food counter and observe the patients eating their meals. They don't talk to the patient but are there 'in case a patient chokes and they have to apply the Heimlich method'.

Office, The: For the nurses, this is the hub of their 'activity'. Equipped with a large window overlooking the 'day room' (and consequently a lot of the patients); with a split-screen CCT system for strategic total-ward oversight and with a library of files (the notes), one for each patient, they sit. Apart for giving out tablets and sorting the odd incident, the nurses virtually can see out their whole shift, without moving from the office. "Blame management".

Old Folks: Heather House Smoking Shed: This is an old folks Ward in the Orthopaedic Hospital in Cork, where the smokers are forced to go outside, winter-or-summer, if they want to smoke. The 'shelter' is a galvanised, one- sided windbreak, in a high part of the city where the wind can be fast and furious. This is slow euthanasia.

Other Effects: If you are taking a tablet to cause effect 'A', it will undoubtedly cause result 'B' and others as well.

Paranoia: A feeling which can be registered by the patient, on foot of the psych's penetrating questions. Ostensibly the PE exists to relieve emotional distress; quite often it causes it through insensitivity. Closed questions, with yes or no answers, are the mainstay, of PE-PC interaction. This, possibly in the name of 'efficiency'. (There are more patients, along the corridor, waiting to be seen). But "Do you hear voices"- type questions can irritate the patient.

Patient Dynamics: Personal space, 'on the ward' is quite limited and the social dynamic is one of constant encounter with virtual strangers; this in the name of healing.

Patient Community and Social Networking: Social networking tools are a central feature of the integrity of the PC

Patient Friendships: Many encounters (hardly friendships) occur in hospital. The thing you don't want (but can't avoid) is when, later, this guy you don't recognise comes up to you on the bus, and, in a loud voice, says, "Oh, I met you in the mental hospital!".

PC and Volunteerism: It's now got to the point where, if you want to work for someone, free of charge, (just to keep your hand in) you have to go to a specialist organisation (a sort of clearing house), with your CV, and do an interview before being referred to an 'employer' for another interview; before you get on the shop -floor. We're that far from full-employment.

PE - Psychiatric Establishment: It has gone through years of training in the pursuit of knowledge and lifestyle. Give them as much of a miss as you can.

PE and Conditioning: Conditioning is like modifying a computers operating system. Through a process of tight questioning, the psych attempts to download your apps; get to your central processor and to your operating system (which is deemed to be inadequate for purpose).

PE and Internationalism: International Travel; the World Economy; Irish psychs following the money out of the country and others from poor countries coming into this country, constitute part of the PE Internationalism process which we are witnessing at present. It's all about money.

PE and PC; Detachment: The PE appears very detached from the PC and it is recommended that the PC adopt the same strategy. Independent living starts in the moment.

PE and the State: The PE is empowered by the State to lock you up if it sees fit, i.e. if it doesn't like your act. You can try to be respectful of them, in the 'clinic', but this may not make a difference; it's like going before the parole board and being turned down, with no explanation; a Kafkaesque situation.

PE and Voice Quality; Male: It is a characteristic of some male psychs that they speak in a loud voice and start the proceedings immediately you are in the door of their offices. This is to establish dominance in the 'interaction'.

PE and World Knowledge: For those on heavy medication, it can be hard to keep up with the news. Psychs will even check you on that. Tell them you don't watch the news because it's too negative.

PE as Teachers: for reasons of manners and mores the PE are clinicians, not teachers.

PE Radical Tablet Monopoly: The Pharma-Psycho-Nursing triangle has a radical monopoly over the manufacture, prescription and dispensation of tablets. It is a huge triangle and very stable as all triangles are.

PE/PC Dynamics: Some members of the PC are virtually inert due to heavy sedation. In 'his office', the psych adopts an inert posture also; in the cause of professional conduct.

PE: Strangers: While you won't be a stranger to your psych, your psych will be a stranger to you due to the uni-directional nature of the information flow between you. You are better off not knowing them, or anything about them; give them a wide berth unless absolutely necessary

Personality, Spirit, Self Esteem and Confidence: can all be destroyed by tablets. Respect for Individual Dignity is vital, (both for macro and micro reasons) and this ought to be reflected in our therapies.

Pharmaceutical Corporations: The trans-national network of tablet manufacturers, which forms the base of the PE triangle; very closely allied to the other two node points: psychiatry and nursing.

Philosophy of Healing: Who is the healed person? The person who functions optimally; it's hard to function optimally on Valium.

Phone, Nurses, the: It used be that if one knocked on the office door, to get a nurse's attention for some business, the answer would be: "I'm on the phone". Ten minutes later, while a clearly friendly chat proceeded inside, one would get the attention one wanted. Things have changed somewhat.

Physical Force/Restraint: There is a huge difference between two nurses holding onto patient's upper arms, until 'he' cools down; and three nurses and two security men kneeling on 'his' ribs, causing significant bruising to achieve the same result. Both of these events are documented (or should be) but they are worlds apart; the difference between non-violent and violent behaviour.

Pick Ups; Attendant Emotions: If you are picked up by the Guards, don't make a scene. They don't care about you; to them, it's just a job.

Plain Speech: There is talk about 'changing the language around Mental Health Care'. It's happened before. 'Lunatic' is no longer part of the vernacular. The goal is Sanity and stigmatic terms get in the way.

Positivity: To look on the positive side; if you flip out, there is somewhere to go and be fed and kept. It's a very hard trip which is why people in there want to get out as soon as possible.

Poverty Trap: Austerity plus. Most members of the PC are on €203 per week 'Disability' Allowance. Denied a job, in most cases; hard to make ends meet.

Powerlessness: Can infect the person within the ward. It's important to make good friends and to get out, regularly, even if on small trips.

Pregnancy and Lithium: Some drugs affect a woman's ability to have healthy babies.

Private Practice: Good for a top-up.

Productive Orientation, The: Term coined by Erich Fromm, in his book, 'The Sane Society' to designate the attitude of the sane person.

Productivity, lack of: The PC lacks the opportunity for productivity and the dignity (as well as money) it brings. There are a number of therapy centres in the Republic. It is not beyond the imagination of therapists and others to design products which could be made, for sale, by people with emotional health issues.

Professional Guillotine: This is the point beyond which the PE refuses to socially engage the PC

Professional Language: Obscure to the layperson.

Professionalisation of Values: 'Whenever a value is recognised by Society a new profession grows around it, eventually consuming most of the funds allocated to promulgating that value and thereby, inhibiting its attainment.' Discuss.

Provocateurs: Parts of the PC would be further ahead in their political organisation if some members took it easy and listened to the consensus.

Psychiatrists, a Guild: The chief characteristic of a Guild is that it is self-regulating. A secondary facet is that it limits the number of acolytes whom it selects and trains.

Psychiatry: A subtle business but not rocket science; otherwise we would all be in orbit which is not what it wants.

Psychiatry and Telepathy: Psychiatry is a 'philosophy' whose core belief is that matter is the highest reality. So don't go talking to them about the existence of telepathy or you will be inside in two shakes of a lamb's tail.

Psychic Tai Chi: This is what mainly goes on between nurses and patients, and the nurses must win, in all cases; otherwise things can get fractious. Choose your encounters carefully.

Put Downs: The delicate PC soul is easily put down. The PE knows this.

Queues: Queuing is an ubiquitous part of life on the ward; queuing for: Breakfast, Dinner and Tea; Coffee;

`Meds; and Consultations. During these times, life becomes linear and patience becomes a virtue.

Quiet Room: A good idea for meditation and silence, unless someone else comes in, which happens frequently. How's about a 'Do Not Disturb' sign?

Quote: from a nurse to a suffering patient: "Objectively, you are not depressed". 'nuff said.

Reality, Authentic and Inauthentic: The experience of receiving a stigma can be very unnerving. It's like having the carpet pulled from under one's perceptions; one's belief system and ones world. It's like your human credibility is being taken away. It's like being told there is authentic and inauthentic reality, and the latter is yours. This is where support of understanding friends is very important.

Reality, Compartmentalisation of: Reality is so vast and so deep that, in order to try and get a handle on (some) of it, we deconstruct it into bits and bytes; words and sentences; concepts; strings of concepts and areas of expertise. (Vocations). The PC has its area of expertise also

Regional Teams: As (if) 'A Vision for Change' is 'rolled out' you may go before a multi-professional team to be 'assessed' and given a 'care plan' which will be a menu for your life. Will you be included in the design of the details? Will they include a job? We wonder.

Rest: When you are not living in 'the sea of tranquility' and your inner world is tense and tired, go lie down, for a while.

Revolving Door Syndrome: The syndrome whereby some people return to hospital, again and again. The reason given by nurses is that these people stopped taking their tablets, (which is probably true). The subtext is that some tablets are so unpleasant that people give them up, feel better; stay off them and go back on the same old loop again.

Sanity and the Environment: There is evidence that 'environmental factors' can play a significant part in fostering Mental Ill-Health. Which leads to the question: Does the Irish College of Psychiatrists make any input to Government on environmental proposals, like Town Planning? Building Standards? or Rent Policy?

Sanity/Insanity: have social and cultural overtones and the PE need to take these into account.

Scrunch or be Scrunched: from Charles Dickens. If you don't want to, or can't, 'scrunch', then settle for naming, lest you be named. Accuracy and compassion are necessary, which gives you plenty of scope.

Secrecy and the PE: Confidentiality is another word for it. That's fair enough when it's your business and you don't want it discussed outside the ward. However, you also have to accept that the PE will not discuss its business with you, under any circumstances; a bit of a party stopper but that's it.

Serial Junior Doctors: It seems that serial junior doctors are both here today and gone tomorrow. They sit-in on out-clinics; ask the same questions you have heard a thousand times and never change the 'meds'. Then they disappear without trace. They didn't know you, in the first place; they still don't know you; just a page on the notes. Your head was a rung on their career ladder and they rose upon it. Did they say thank you for the free trip? Probably not.

Service Users: The word 'user' has negative connotations but patience is a virtue.

Sexuality and Libido: Some tablets quell the libido and obviously, an active sex-life. This may be of less concern to the PE than you think. It may be more concerned with maintaining the status quo than in your fecundity.

Shaking: One of the commonest forms of secondary, or 'side' effects of PE drugs; Lithium in this case. The common response of the PE to this is to administer another drug, 'Akineton', which partly resolves the situation.

Shock and Awe: Experienced, when they come to take you away.

Skill Sharing: Practiced by the members of The Basement Resource Centre and 'The Next Step' in Cork.

Sleep: Essential for optimal functioning and clear head.

Slí Eile: Complementary Live-In Mental Health Community.

Smoking Shelter, The: This is an outdoor, Perspex, bus-shelter-like edifice where the patient smokers gather to puff and talk; even at night, in winter. It shouldn't be there, in the first place as the Law provides for indoor smoking in Mental Health Centres.

Social Contact: In Carraig Mor lock-up facility, in Cork, patients are forced to hand over their mobile phones, thus depriving them of contact with family and friends, something which could help their mental health. Access to a land line is discretionary. Is this legal?.

 Social Grace and Tablets: Many sedatives can significantly reduce the recipient's social grace and thereby confer pariah status upon them in Society.

Social Media and PC: A source of cohesion to the PC is the array of social networking tools now available.

Social Space: Studies probably have been done on the amount of space humans require on a continuing basis, to feel comfortable.

Social Welfare, PC and Extra Work: It is possible for people on Disability Allowance to work on a limited basis and not lose their benefit.

Society, You and the Law: Your position, within the ward may be due to the Law in action, but from common observation, the Law can sometimes be an ass.

Solutions: Conventional wisdom, within the PE is that 'independent living' is the way to go. Some prefer community settings, provided they are homely, with a fair dollop of sharing and caring and their preference needs to be respected. Appropriate work is mandatory for proper healing both emotionally and economically.

Song, Elation and Context: It may be 'acceptable' to sing with the choir, in church, or at the match when one's team has scored, but it is not appropriate to sing, walking along Patrick' Street on one's own, at five in the morning. It's a matter of context.

Speak One's Truth to Power: An edict which has come down the centuries for those who are experiencing an imbalance of power.

Speak Your Mind: A middle- of the- road, high quality, magazine which came out of St Catherine's Ward, St Finbarr's Hospital, Cork City, now issues from The Next Step.

Speed of Thought: Impaired by lots of tablets

Stigma: At present, there is a quiet revolution going on in this country around the issue of Mental Health, and you can be part of it: more acceptance, more understanding, more participation.

Stigma, Corporate Identity of a Sub-Culture: It's the antithesis of a halo. Those who wear it hang out together for ratification and support. This represents un-used labour as well as poor therapy.

Stigma/Diagnosis: In the PC-PE World they are identical events and as a result the recipient descends and the donor ascends in the eyes of the world. A dishonourable social arrangement.

Stratification pays: Remember, it was the slaves who built the pyramids, but eventually they found the Promised Land. However, who wants to be a slave?

Stress of hospital: It is arguable whether the ward induces more or less stress. Survivors don't usually argue that point; they feel the former is true and no-one wants to go back.

Student Nurses: Usually very sociable and 'chatty' with the patients; they have no administrative work to do. As time goes by, when they return, qualified, they will be putting more of their attention into the paperwork and will be seen less-and-less by their 'charges'.

Suicide and Medication: The point has been made that unfortunate people, who take their own lives, are not checked for the presence of psychotropic drugs, in their bloodstream.

Swimming Upstream: A term to denote the emotional position of someone who has the deep blues; or who is on heavy downer medication.

Tablets and Care: On the ward, the only time you will talk to a psychiatrist will be during two, 5 -10min. windows per week, in his office. That's where tablets are 'discussed'. Psychiatrists don't hang out in patient's space; they do in Scotland.

Tablets and Charisma: Tablets can strip people of their charisma and lessen the chances of their social bonding.

Tablets, Addiction to: a problem with many drugs is that they are addictive; that's one of the reasons it's hard to come off.

Talk Therapy: Increasingly, as the confessional has all but been supplanted, 'talk therapy' is being resorted to as a means of 'getting it off one's chest' and learning coping skills. The PE externalises this service as it doesn't believe much in listening to the details.

Transcendence: Sometimes you can feel transcendent. The PE won't relate to your transcendence, but it does relate to Transnationals

Undue Process: In the nineteenth century, family members could be committed to Lunatic Asylums because they were surplus to economic requirements at home. With the advent of the medical profession, theirs became the prerogative as to whether or not to commit a person to such incarceration. With the advent of psychotropic drugs in the 1940/50s a life sentence was no longer deemed necessary. However the word of the medic was, and still is, final, in deciding if a candidate (referred by the family, a guard or a member of the public) should be taken into a recognised medical centre.